E|F

exposed
& FEARLESS

vinny

To D'Ann,

Be Afraid,

It's OK!

grosso

To D'Ann,

a friend,

It's OK!

waterfront press

a division of enview designs
Las Vegas, Nevada

exposed
& FEARLESS
3rd edition

vinny grosso

ISBN-13: 978-0692140994
ISBN-10: 0692140999

dedication

To Dick Jackman, my public relations professor at Villanova University, who taught me perhaps my most valuable lesson for life: when it rains, I let it.

about the cover

The cover is a close up image of the face of Michelangelo's *David*, tightly cropped and partially tinted red. I love the facial expression on the *David*, it actually changes depending on the direction you look at it and how it is cropped. I also felt the *David* was the ideal icon for this book. The *David* is *exposed* in several meanings of the word and *FEARLESS* as he prepares for battle with Goliath.

special thanks to...

for making the book possible:

David R Goodsell
editor

Meghan Toner
T. Gene Hatcher

for making me possible:

Sandra & Michael Grosso

for making me the most fortunate person in the world...ever:

My Family - siblings, in-laws, aunts, uncles, nieces, nephews, a whole bunch of incredible cousins and a few special friends who feel like family

forward

For a magician, Vinny Grosso is not terribly interested in keeping secrets. He is an open book. If you find yourself lucky enough to get invited to a dinner party at his home in Las Vegas, be prepared for stories of his full-body laser hair removal, or his latest dating escapades (which, really, should be compiled into another book, also titled 'exposed and fearless').

Normally, this full disclosure from a new acquaintance may seem too forward, but Vinny's authenticity, rooted in honesty and self-deprecating humor, can be contagious. As a result, many of the fascinating and wildly successful people that have come across Vinny's path have been willing, in turn, to be open with him and share the stories that fill the following pages.

The idea of studying the success of others is not original but it is, in my opinion, undervalued. With this book, Vinny has done us the favor of compiling a series of case studies examining some of the country's most talented and successful performers. While most of us are content to put these individuals on a pedestal and admire their talent from a distance, Vinny has invited us to take a closer look at the habits and beliefs that contribute to their success. And, unlike a journalist who may spend a few hours interviewing his or her subjects, Vinny's position as President of The Society of American Magicians and his work as a Tour Manager has provided him with the unique opportunity to spend hundreds of hours living and traveling with these subjects.

Colin Mochrie & Brad Sherwood, Cesar Millan, and the other individuals that you will read about in this book will probably never publish personal improvement books of their own. So, we're lucky that Vinny has captured some of their lessons in these pages. It would be impossible in a book of this size to distill all of the factors that contributed to their success, but Vinny has 'skimmed the creme' for us, handing us a handful of insights that we can choose to employ as we work towards own goals.

- Michael Mills
CEO Mills Entertainment

table of contents

chapter 1

Why Write this Book?

...*or any book?*

If you knew me when I was younger, that is a question you would be asking. I have worked very hard on my writing skills since joining the professional ranks, but it was a rough beginning.

When I was in elementary school I was placed in a remedial writing class and the remedial writing teacher was my mother. I, along with four other kids, was singled out as needing help with my writing skills. I really didn't understand why I was in this group. I was, by my own assessment, a brilliant writer. I could see, however, why the other kids were in this class. They clearly needed help, help way beyond writing skills, like help distinguishing the difference between paste and lunch. But me? Why was I in this class???

My mother explained my presence in her class to others by saying, "Vincent thinks faster than he can write. So his stories jump around because, by the time he writes down one thought, his mind is four or five thoughts ahead." You have to love a mom who explains your need for remedial help as a result of your gifted mind. By the way, I usually was referred to as "Vincent" in situations like this and others, such as not having my room clean, or not finishing my vegetables.

I would love to think she was right about my "gifted mind," but I have a history of being a poor writer beyond elementary school. When I was in high school, for some reason I took AP English. On the AP exam I scored the lowest possible score; you know, the score they give you for showing up and spelling your name correctly. If I recall correctly there were two essays. I knew I bombed the first one but the second one asked to write about a humorous author. I wrote about myself, citing that it was humorous that I had no clue how to write. Apparently the examiners did not find it humorous.

In college I studied mechanical engineering at Villanova University. I chose engineering for several reasons. I was good at math, I enjoyed figuring out how things worked, and I did not want to have to write a paper in college. I almost got away with that last part. Until my senior year the only writing I had to do was for a freshman class in literature for engineers - literature class in name only. We didn't want to be there and I don't think the teacher got much joy out of working with us. We all did what we had to and moved on.

My junior year of college was tough on me and my GPA. I did not want to take any more engineering classes than I had to. The only way to reduce the number of engineering classes was to have a minor. At that time I was convinced after college I was going to be the next David Copperfield, so I chose a minor that would help with that goal.

I thought theatre would be the best choice. The acting classes looked like fun, but there were also requirements that called for writing and studying literature, two activities that made the alternative of sitting in a class with mostly guys discussing finite element analysis a little more appealing.

Communications!

My experience with communication majors was that they were always discussing their social life, and were never too concerned about classes. There were lots of options for classes, so I was sure I'd be able to choose a curriculum where I didn't have to write. That was almost the case. One of the required classes for a communications minor was "Survey of Communications," and the syllabus said that only two written papers were required.

That was almost a deal breaker, but my friends in Communications assured me that they weren't difficult or demanding papers. It was a freshman class and would be easy, even for me. I was also able to convince the chair of the department to allow me to take a couple theater classes as part of my communications minor. They essentially customized a minor for me, knowing that I wanted to pursue magic as a career. Because they were so accommodating, I figured two papers would be a sufficient trade off for escaping a senior year filled with engineering classes.

That was quite possibly the single best decision I made in college. The classes were all relevant and surprisingly fun! I don't want to say the classes were easy but compared to Stress Analysis and Machine Design classes I took the year before, these classes didn't even seem like college. They were social gatherings where we shared our opinions. You had to say something incredibly stupid to be "wrong," and even then, professors would try to relate to your point.

In the world of engineering there seemed to be right and wrong answers which were absolute. If I was wrong I was told I was wrong, and I felt like professors enjoyed pointing out I was wrong. My minor in Communications wasn't just a curriculum change, it was a culture change. That became even more obvious when I got back my first paper. Remember, this was my first written paper since my freshman year. I felt good about it, just like I had when I was in elementary school. It was a masterpiece. In fact, I fantasized that the professor would tell me I didn't need to show up the rest of the semester. He would acknowledge my expertise, so why should I waste my time. He'd just give me an A. So you will understand that I was excited to see my grade and read the wonderful comments he would write about my insights and perspectives. As he handed back the papers, I wore an irrepressible grin from ear to ear.

Irrepressible?

I got a C on the paper! How was that possible? Was he even a real professor? How did he even get a Ph.D.? This was ridiculous and unacceptable. I immediately sought him out during his office hours. He had some explaining to do. How dare he give my masterpiece a C, and who was he to judge anyway?

Although he understood that I wanted to know why my work was worth only a C, I think he was a little surprised that I was so passionate about it. After all, it was only a small paper that counted very little towards my final grade. He asked us to write about a, b and c and explain x, y and z. I said to him, "Look, here's a, b and c and x, y and z are explained here. How is this not an A?" His response startled me. He explained, "While you have all the elements I asked for, that's all you have. You didn't embellish them at all." I replied with, "You mean I didn't give you enough B.S.?" To which he said, "Well, yes."

I had just spent three years in engineering learning how to identify and eliminate unnecessary information from a problem in order to find a clear solution. Now I had to introduce unnecessary information to give the appearance that I knew the solution. Despite not wanting to be an engineer, I felt more comfortable thinking like one. But these were the rules of the game and despite my deflated ego, I was motivated to win.

Writing the second paper for that class I had no delusions it was a masterpiece. The vision of the professor lauding me with compliments was gone; in fact I was a bit angry writing it. I muttered to myself, "If it's B.S. he wants, it's B.S. he'll get!" When I handed in my paper, I thought "This isn't me, but I think it's what you want."

I got an A. I'm still not one hundred percent sure he gave me an A because it was A material or if he wanted to avoid another "discussion." Regardless of the reason, that was my last college paper and I was thrilled it was over.

My aversion to literature was not just writing, I really did not like to read. Even now I cannot open a book and read for more than a few minutes before I lose focus and attention. I have never read a book of fiction. Not since Dr. Seuss. I have read a few nonfiction books, and if listening to books on tape counts, a few more. All non-fiction. Contrary to what one might expect of a non-reader, I rarely watch television or go to the movies.

So why in the world would I write a book?

The subject matter in this book is important to me. It covers topics that have broad appeal, stories of successful people and the role of fear in their journey to success. The subject matter is also very personal. Each chapter is about someone I know personally and my observations from spending time with them. Each one is uniquely amazing and I consider myself lucky to know them.

In my pursuit of becoming a magician, I became involved with The Society of American Magicians, the oldest and most prestigious magic organization in the world. Harry Houdini served as president from 1917 until his death in 1926. In 2011, I served as president, too, making that the one and only correlation between us. I obviously didn't know Harry Houdini, but my involvement with the magic community has introduced me to many equally incredible, interesting and amazing people.

I also do work for a production company, Mills Entertainment, and tour manage several different types of live shows. I know many of the artists I work with well, and when on the road we have had our share of conversations about life and its challenges.

Despite my efforts to not be an engineer, I have a consulting and software business in the interior window coverings industry. I have patents in my name and travel the world meeting interesting people in that field.

Recently I had an eye exam, I was told I have perfect vision, but difficulty focusing. I shared this assessment with my brother, he asked if that was an eye exam or a personal assessment! I like doing a lot of things. I like exploring different places, experiencing other cultures and learning about other people. There have been a lot of benefits. My life has been amazing, I enjoy every minute of it, and it has been enriched by the people I have gotten to know.

With this great vision and deficient focus there are some consequences. I am not going to be the next David Copperfield or anyone else that I am writing about in this book. However, I'm not convinced that's a bad thing.

I am writing this book to help me figure out my future. By following along, perhaps you will find some answers to your own questions. It's easy to admire people's accomplishments and fantasize about the rewards of their labors, but I am exploring what it takes to achieve them. Did they make deals with the devil? Are they just lucky? Did they make sacrifices? What obstacles did they encounter? What motivated them? Were they ever afraid?

I am writing this book about a few of my friends who have inspired me and motivated me. Because of them I aspire to do more with my life. When you read about them, I hope they will have the same effect on you.

chapter 2

exposed

exposed how?

The word "exposed" has a few meanings, a couple of which apply to this book, a couple of which that don't, and I'm sure while that's a relief to some, it will disappoint a few, too. The first meaning is as an *introduction*. I am exposing you to people, and perhaps to aspects of their lives of which you are not aware. The second meaning is as a *reveal*, I will expose how these people have achieved or accomplished some incredible things.

Several of the people in this book are household names, that you have already been exposed to from television or other media. You *know of them*, but you likely don't really *know them*. In my time spent with these people I have seen aspects of their lives and personalities that one never sees on television. As is often the case, the "hidden" attributes of these people will surely surprise you.

There are some people in this book who are very well known within the magic community, but not as much by the general public. Regardless of whether you already know them or not, I am sure you will learn something new, look at them in a new light, and find them just as inspiring as I do.

This book also includes people whom I'm sure you have never met or heard of before. We all have some people like this in our lives, people who have done and do amazing things under the radar. Often times their humility is more impressive than what they have actually done.

The exposure you are probably most interested in is the "how." I don't like surprises, I don't like secrets being kept from me, and I don't like unsolved problems. I always want to know how something is done. Not knowing the "how" actually reduces my enjoyment or appreciation of something. Some people like the wonder of not knowing. They're not only content with the mystery, they find it gratifying. Definitely not me! If you can watch a show that ends with a cliff hanger, and be content to wait until the next show is released, this may not be a good book for you.

I will be pulling back the curtain on my friends in this book, but not like a masked magician who exposes age old secrets of magic. You will not be learning the secrets of how David Copperfield made the Statue of Liberty vanish; you will learn, in essence, *how* David Copperfield was able to make the Statue of Liberty vanish, how he put himself in position to pull off the most famous illusion of our time.

I have always been impressed by the activities that lead to a particular accomplishment, much more so than the actual accomplishment itself. When we read or hear about someone doing an extraordinary act, our initial reaction is to marvel at it. But what about what it took to get there?

We celebrate a team for winning the Super Bowl and then focus on their performance in that one game. We may have seen some of the games they played in the playoffs, but how often do we hear about all they did in training camp and during the off season that put them in a position to win the Super Bowl? Without these activities, a Super Bowl victory never happens. These are the things I want to learn. These are the things I want to know how to do.

But it's the Super Bowl victory that gets our attention, isn't it? We live in a society that focuses on the end result and thereby fails to learn some of life's most important lessons. The old adage "winning isn't everything" was wise because people used to value the preparation for winning as much as the win itself. These stories are about both.

What do you learn about how a team won a Super Bowl by only studying that game? Do you really know how they did it if you have no idea what it took to get them there?

As I explore how these people do what they do, a quote frequently comes to mind: "It took me ten years to become an overnight success." Variations of it have been attributed to many people, and for many it really is the true secret to success. Everyone in this book, "paid their dues," put in the work to become who they are.

Other quotes that come to mind are Seneca's "Luck is what happens when preparation meets opportunity," and Louis Pasteur's "Chance favors the prepared mind." An underlying theme in this book is that success follows hard work. In this book we will expose the details of hard work, preparation, chance, and opportunity in the lives of a few special people. It is this type of exposure that *exposed & FEARLESS* is truly about.

chapter 3

FEARLESS

is anyone truly fearless?

From one of my favorite movies, *My Cousin Vinny*, imagine Marisa Tomei using a harsh yet somehow sweet, Brooklyn accent to describe the following:

"Imagine you're a deer. You're prancing along. You get thirsty. You spot a little brook. You put your little deer lips down to the cool, clear water. BAM! A f—in' bullet rips off part of your head! Your brains are laying on the ground in little bloody pieces! Now I ask you: Would you give a f— what kind of pants the son of a b—- who shot you was wearing?!"

Now I ask you, was that deer afraid? Was that deer afraid to put his little deer lips down to the cool, clear water in the presence of a man with a rifle and, no doubt, leather pants? Nope. But, why not?

I give a talk every year at Rensselaer Polytechnic Institute on getting over your fears. I use a scenario similar to the one Marisa Tomei described to illustrate my points on fear. Mine, however, involves a wolf and an animal trap instead of the deer and fashion conscious hunter. I describe this scenario using an actual animal trap!

Mine goes like this: "A wolf is prancing along the forest." I'm not sure wolves prance, but that really doesn't matter. I use a plastic fork to represent the prancing wolf, moving it gracefully towards the animal trap. "He spots a free meal just sitting out in the open. He looks around and does not see anyone, so he grabs it." I place the fork into the trap, triggering it. "Wham, the wolf is caught!" The fork shatters as the jaws of the trap violently close.

I ask the same question, was the wolf afraid? The wolf had no fear because he had no knowledge or experience with the animal trap. To him it looked like a free lunch, so why not grab it? Without knowledge and without experience you are fearless, but this can also be dangerous.

If we introduce knowledge into the equation, the scenario becomes far less dangerous. However, the wolf now becomes fearful. If the wolf has knowledge of what the trap is designed to do, he will likely not reach for the "free meal," and avoid it entirely. His fear, a result of knowledge of the situation, will drive him away.

If you could explain to the wolf that the trap is designed to crush a single paw, but if the force of the jaws is distributed over a wider surface area it won't cause nearly as much pain, and the paw can easily slide out, the wolf will still fear it. The wolf will have that fear until he has not only the knowledge of the trap, but experience, too.

The first time you try something, despite your knowledge and preparation, there is always a level of fear. It is only through experience combined with knowledge that fear is reduced. This is a much healthier scenario for fearlessness than that of the wolf in the beginning where he had neither knowledge nor experience of the trap, and lost his paw.

Having some level of fear is a good thing. A skydiver friend once told me that accidents rarely happen to newer skydivers. It's usually the very experienced and knowledgeable skydivers that have accidents. Why? Because they have very little fear. They push limits and can become over confident with their preparation. Similar stories are told of really strong, experienced swimmers drowning or seasoned skiers crashing into trees. A lack of fear can create hazardous situations even for those with a great deal of knowledge and tremendous experience.

We often equate fear to weakness. If you are afraid of a bully it is because you are weak. I couldn't disagree with that equation more. People are afraid of bullies because their knowledge of bullies is that they can do damage if we do not do what they say. There is no experience to either reinforce that perception or prove it wrong. Fear comes not from weakness but from knowledge, or limited knowledge, lacking experience.

The bully has fear too, but from a different perspective. The bully has experience and no knowledge. His experience is that acting in a forceful way causes people to go along with him. He knows no other way to accomplish his goals and is afraid if he acts differently he may be challenged. His initial response to a challenge is, more than likely, to be more aggressive.

The fear for both parties in this scenario can certainly be overwhelming. I am not suggesting this level of fear is a good thing. There are levels of fear that I think are good for you. As you read the chapters ahead, all of the people in this book have learned to manage their fears. In some cases fear has been a primary motivator. In other cases, it has been an obstacle, the overcoming of which has separated that person from the crowd. As incongruent as it may seem, fear should play a role in our lives. Show me a fearless person and I guarantee there's a tragic story.

Of course the title of this book, *exposed & FEARLESS*, is meant to get your attention. I believe that true fearlessness is dangerous and not a viable goal. Having fear is good as long as the fear does not have you. Some might want to equate fear to healthy respect for any sort of danger or negative consequence, not something to avoid, but rather something to use to advantage, to push yourself beyond what you thought you knew you were capable of.

chapter 4

Can Cesar Millan Really

Whisper To Dogs?

exposed

When people find out I have worked with Cesar Millan they generally have two reactions. The most common is "Oh my gosh, I LOVE him!" The other is, "Does he really talk to the dogs?" I'm never surprised by the first reaction. People are crazy about their dogs, so anyone as gifted as Cesar in rehabilitating dogs is sure to warm the hearts of many. He also has a magnanimous personality. This is evident when you see him on television and is the same in real life.

The second reaction always causes me to do a quick psychoanalysis of the person who asked. Do they actually think Cesar says to a hyper-active, salivating pit bull with its canines on full display, "Psst, come over here," then cups his hand to the side of his mouth, leans over to the ear of the dog and says, "I think you should stop salivating and relax, everyone around you is getting nervous." Do they think the pit bull instantly stops, looks back at Cesar and, in a telepathic way, says to Cesar, "Sorry about that, my owner made it too easy for me to act that way. I'll behave now."

As crazy as that sounds, I have come to realize the very last part is actually true. Cesar knows how to communicate with dogs. He does not whisper to them, in fact he rarely uses verbal commands. Cesar uses his presence and his energy to let the dogs know exactly what is acceptable and what is not.

Are you doing a quick psychoanalysis on me? That is probably advisable, but not because of what I just told you about Cesar. A concept difficult for us to understand is how our energy impacts our interactions with other living things. This is not a big revelation; it is a point Cesar emphasizes in his television show, his books, his live shows and in his training classes.[1]

It is very difficult for most people to understand and internalize, primarily because energy is not a tangible, quantitative quality. Or is it? One of the most powerful moments in Cesar's live show is when he shares his secret of energy with the audience.

Cesar explains to the audience that the concept of energy is foreign to most people. Performers, like musicians, comedians, and actors, understand it. They experience it

---

[1] Cesar offers clinics and training courses at his Dog Psychology Center on 45 acres in the rolling hills of Santa Clarita, California (just outside Los Angeles). www.cesarsway.com

every time they step on stage, but they, too, find it difficult to explain and seemingly impossible to measure.

Cesar recounts a conversation with a doctor friend of his about the concept of energy and the challenge of expressing this to his clients. As with most difficult problems, the best solution is generally a simple one. In this case it was a heart rate monitor.

To demonstrate the importance of energy, Cesar filmed a video which shows a heart rate monitor attached to a dog, Brazil, and another one to the dog's owner, Jill. A third is attached to Cesar. In the first example Brazil's and Jill's heart rates are monitored as another dog walks by.

Jill's heart rate spikes as the other dog approaches which causes Brazil's heart rate to spike. The result is a lot of barking and aggressive behavior. The more Jill's heart rate increases, the more Brazil's does, and the wilder Brazil acts.

Jill then hands Brazil over to Cesar who takes a deep breath, releasing tension in his body. We can see Brazil respond, becoming calmer. This is verified by the heart rate monitors.

The real test is when the other dog is introduced to Brazil. Will Cesar's heart rate increase? How will Brazil respond?

Cesar remains calm and confident as the other dog approaches, maintaining a normal heart rate. Brazil follows Cesar's lead and does not get excited, does not bark, and is not aggressive.

Amazingly, Brazil's heart rate mirrored his handler's, although the two situations were just moments apart. This is a big "ah-ha" moment in Cesar's live show, and one can really sense that the audience is beginning to understand what Cesar is talking about.

Near the beginning of his show Cesar says, "I train people and rehabilitate dogs." The dogs are not the problem, they are simply reacting to their environment. Although the audience agrees, I don't think they fully comprehend it.

Cesar is a talented storyteller and spends a good portion of the first half of his live show telling stories to illustrate this point. His stories are highly entertaining and great theatre, true stories of past clients, including Oprah, in situations with which we are all familiar, usually first hand stories about the introduction of a new dog to a cat, the peepy-poopy walk, or the treatment of a dog as a member of the family.

These stories are all told in a light-hearted, humorous way, but there is an important message in each of them. The majority of the audience is guilty of doing the things that Cesar highlights in his stories. Since everyone is laughing together as Cesar acts out a situation, I'm not convinced it registers to the audience members that, "Wait, maybe what I'm doing is not the best thing for my dog." But perhaps that is not too important at this point.

This is, after all, a live show, and people want to be entertained. What Cesar does in the first part of the show *is* entertainment; but he also lays a foundation. In the second half of the show he drives these points home with examples like the heart rate monitor video of Brazil.

So, can Cesar Millan really talk to dogs? Are you convinced yet? Well his fans are...and anyone that has fans has critics. The most popular retort from Cesar's critics is that he uses fancy editing. How many takes were needed to get that segment right? What went on off camera to get the dog to behave?

It's for these reasons I love Cesar's live show. There are no edits, there are no off-camera moments. What you see is what you get. I know this may not seem so impressive since I have only described Cesar entertaining his audiences with poignant stories and commentating on prerecorded video. But as true showmen are taught, Cesar saves his best for last - dog demonstrations.

Dog demonstrations are live demonstrations with dogs from a local shelter or rescue that have behavioral issues in need of correcting. Cesar will usually do three or four of these in a show. Since every show uses different dogs, every show is different.

That said, there are some common problem behaviors found in dogs from most shelters and rescues. For example, pulling hard on the leash. Of course, there are behavioral issues that are not appropriate for a live show format; severe aggression being one of them. Such behavior takes time and multiple sessions to work out.

I'll never forget the first of Cesar's live shows I saw. The first dog came out pulling his handler behind him. I cannot recall the dog's name, but I definitely recall his muscular neck, clearly developed from years of dragging his handler wherever he wanted to go. However, when Cesar put his leash on the dog and took control, the tugging instantly disappeared. The dog transformed right before our eyes, as if he were hypnotized and we were mesmerized.

How did he do it? Energy certainly played a role, as in the example of Brazil. Cesar became the alpha, as we're so accustomed to hearing, and was instantly in charge. He was a perfect example of the phrase he has popularized, "calm and assertive." We could see those attributes in action.

Cesar uses other techniques to ensure command over dogs, like placing the leash high, towards the head where the dog can sense it, making sure he leads the way when he walks a dog so that the dog follows. These things reinforce an assertive rapport with any dog. As Cesar explains to his audiences, dogs want to follow; they're looking to be led. However, that leader must be stable, and if not, the dogs can sense that, and instinctively try to compensate by leading themselves. The audience gradually realizes that the lesson is really for the handler, not the dog. This demonstration reinforces Cesar's statement earlier in the show "I train humans and rehabilitate dogs."

The handlers for Cesar's demonstrations are volunteers from shelters and rescues who without question love and care about dogs and have had years of experience handling them. Even so, they often make common mistakes. But Cesar has a charm about him that enables him to be honest and endearing at the same time. The handlers do not resist. They embrace the correction and by the time they leave the stage they are handling their dog like Cesar...well mostly like him, definitely a huge improvement.

Cesar's charm is an outward expression of his energy, which is based on calm, yet assertive behavior. Whether he is working with a dog, a dog handler or owner, or an arena full of fans, he exudes a quiet confidence. He is always unapologetically honest and his motives, to help dogs and owners, are clear. When you add his sense of humor to the equation you get charm.

Cesar's approach to altering inappropriate behavior in dogs is always the same. He is calm but assertive. Of course he has learned many techniques to bring about change - covertly touching a dog on its belly with his foot combined with an audible "tsst," for example. These are all examples of imparting his energy, relaxed and calm, to the dog.

As Cesar's tour manager and technical director for his live shows, I see them from start to finish, beginning at 3:00 in the afternoon on the day of an 8:00 pm show. I see a dozen dogs brought to the venue by local shelters and rescues. I see Cesar briefly meet the various dog handlers and learn about the problems with each dog. He does not interact with the dogs, just observes and then discusses them with Colleen, the dog trainer who travels with the show.

Cesar goes off for sound check, has dinner in his dressing room and attends to other business affairs. He does not spend hours working with the dogs, correcting their behavior prior to the show as his critics might think. Cesar is the real deal! When the dogs are seen on stage, they still exhibit their poor behavior and Cesar corrects them in what seems to me like an instant. I have worked on his show for over a year and have seen at least one hundred misbehaving dogs meet Cesar on stage. He never ceases to amaze me, nor the audience!

FEARLESS

Having the privilege to work with and get to know Cesar Millan, I have recognized two examples of fearlessness critical to his success. The foundation of his methods is his energy. "Calm and Assertive" is not a catchy phrase Cesar throws out to his audience as if he is trying to get them to buy a used car. It is how he lives his life, around dogs or not. It isn't a switch he turns on and off. It is who he is.

It is also who you can be. I regularly go for a run near my house. I encounter several dogs along the way, although not always the same ones. When I first encountered them I said to my self, "remain calm and project that I am a leader." That worked until one of the dogs started barking and charged towards me. I felt my heart rate spike and could tell I was projecting fear. Over time I have been getting much better. My heart rate doesn't spike anymore and my confidence is gaining. I am striving to achieve Cesar Millan's level of energy.

Cesar has so much experience with dogs that nothing surprises him, and he instinctively reacts appropriately. He is fearless because he has knowledge based on his experience; this allows him to be the best in the world at rehabilitating dogs.

Cesar shares a life-changing experience with his show audiences. He came to America from Mexico by jumping the border. Humorously, Cesar refers to this as an "obstacle course." While he makes light of the experience with humor and charm, his energy, we can tell that this experience is an important part of his life.

Imagine leaving your family, traveling to a foreign country where you have no place to stay and can't speak the language, because you believe you'll have a better opportunity to succeed than where you are now? I can't relate to that story directly but his story is the same as that of my great-grandparents who immigrated from Italy.

Remember, fear should play a role in our lives. As scary as the journey ahead seemed to him, in Cesar's mind the alternative was worse. Once Cesar recognized that fear was not a reflection of weakness, but rather of limited knowledge in need of experience, he sought out that experience, his "obstacle course," and became fearless.

parting thoughts

Pulling back the curtain on Cesar Millan we see an incredibly talented and gifted person who really can talk to dogs. There's no secret to it, in fact he wants everyone to do the same. That's why he has written books, does his television show, his live show, and runs a dog psychology center. In his television show there is no fancy editing, he's just as amazing in his live show as on his television shows.

The secret to his success lies in his ability to break down problems and challenges to their basics. We have a tendency to complicate things. Cesar's approach is from nature, where attributes like energy and tension have more importance than a walking vest or kong. I am fortunate he is my friend, and I have had more than one occasion to seek his advice. I am caught up in the complexities of my dilemma, and Cesar breaks it down into basics. He tells me what I need to hear, and not necessarily what I want to hear.

The other secret to Cesar's success is his passion. He did not decided to work with dogs because he thought he would have an opportunity to be on television. He loves dogs. Working with them is his passion, and he has never veered from that. His success is the result. Once he became clear on who he wanted to be, he remained focused, driven and fearless in pursuing that goal.

chapter 5

Is Improv Comedy Really Made up?

exposed

Have you ever been in a conversation with a group of people, made a comment, and have everyone burst out laughing? For most people these moments don't happen all the time. When they do, you feel like taking a page from the playbook of George Costanza in *Seinfeld,* and say "Thank you. Goodnight!" and exit the conversation on a high note. Imagine having to come up with hundreds of these comments every night. That's just what Colin Mochrie and Brad Sherwood of *Whose Line Is It Anyway?* fame do in their live two-man improv show.

Improv comedy is considered by most comedians to be the most difficult and challenging form of comedy to do well. This is not necessarily evident from the perspective of the audience. "Anyone can get up and do it." There are no lines to memorize so you can't practice exactly what you're going to say or do. How hard is that?" Very, that's how hard, and to make it entertaining from beginning to end is the challenge.

Improvisers have to develop special skills. They exercise different parts of their brain. If you have ever gone water skiing, the first time you do it you are incredibly sore the next day. Even if you keep in shape, you are sore because you don't regularly use your muscles in the way water skiing requires. After water skiing for a bit, the post activity soreness goes away. It's the same with your brain.

Colin Mochrie often tells people in interviews that he gravitated towards improv because he doesn't like to memorize lines or spend time in preparation. Colin says this in his typical humble and sometimes self-deprecating manner. However, having worked on Colin and Brad's show for over five years, I can tell you, Colin prepares!

Colin and Brad are constantly preparing, not in conventional ways, and not in the same way, either. They play word games, strategy games, keep up with current events, and are constantly engaged in clever conversations between themselves. They also discuss the show and the different directions it can go, at length.

Their show is always evolving. In improv, sketches are referred to as "games," and the premise is determined by the audience in what is called an "ask for." An "ask for" is associated with a topic. For example, Colin or Brad may "ask for" an occupation or a foreign country, etc. The audience then shouts out whatever comes to mind and they use this in the game.

In the past, Colin and Brad spent considerable time discussing and analyzing what topics would be best for a particular game's "ask for." After a while, they felt that this began to limit the games; they would generally take a similar direction. Everything was still made up on the spot, but there was a level of familiarity.

They decided to change it up and take another risk as performers. The "ask fors" are now on index cards and when they need a topic for a game it is randomly chosen by an audience member. This makes the games much more difficult and requires a higher level of improvisational skill. It also makes the games more exciting for them and the audience.

Think of someone walking across a high wire. It's exciting and there's tension, but there's also a net under him. If he falls, he'll be fine. That same stunt without the use of the net creates more excitement and tension for both the performer and the audience. That's the way Colin and Brad feel with random topics for their "ask fors." They have no idea where the game is going. That excitement produces a much more thrilling performance.

You would think having random topics selected by the audience and the "ask fors" shouted out would be enough to convince people that the show is improvised. It really amazes me that after the show people ask if it was scripted. I wonder if they actually watched the show.

Colin and Brad are incredibly adept at the call back. A call back is a term used in comedy to reference something that happened earlier. A stand up comic will have scripted call backs and will have fine tuned these after hundreds of performances. Colin and Brad make it look effortless to reference in a humorous way some of the actions and comments made by audience members earlier. This is no easy feat and is undoubtedly made up on the spot. Yet, still people ask, "is it really made up?"

YES! IT IS MADE UP!

Colin and Brad want it to be made up. If they didn't they would do stand up. The community of improv comedians is a close one. They are quite friendly and supportive of each other, and they share the common bond of having to be funny on the spot and then be questioned about it when they are done!

There is, however, one game that Colin and Brad do that I can understand the questioning. It's called Crime. This is where one of them puts on headphones, sits on a stool, and faces away from the audience. For the purposes of this explanation, let's say it's Brad, but it changes every night. Brad is unable to hear or see what is going on. Colin then asks the audience to come up with a "crime." These are intentionally crazy, random and long. One example of a crime the audience came up with was:

"Robbed a potato store and shot a Labradoodle in Spallumcheen at Hubert's cow barber and diaper factory with a dark matter ash catcher"

Did I mention they never make sense? That's the point, to be as difficult and challenging a crime as possible. Once Colin gets this from the audience, Brad takes off his head phones and faces the audience. It is now Brad's job to confess to this crime, verbatim, from the clues given to him in Colin's interrogation. It is like the game "Taboo" on steroids.

I can understand people questioning this game because it seems really impossible that they are able to perform it successfully. It is a game I think would take me hours to complete, if I could complete it at all. People often think that the headphones aren't really on and that Brad can hear what's going on.

In the past Brad would leave the theatre with an audience member, who would then vouch that they did not hear anything. Even then, people questioned it. Colin and Brad are resigned to the fact that people will always question it, and use the headphone method because it keeps the show flowing.

I can tell you unequivocally, Brad cannot hear what's going on. I am floored every night when I see them do this. As amazing as that is, it's not the most amazing part of the game. Their banter in clueing and guessing is entertaining and funny from beginning to end. They're not just trying to play the game of clueing and guessing the crime, they are trying to entertain a couple of thousand people every step of the way.

In every show that I have worked with Colin and Brad they have received a standing ovation. There will always be skeptics in the crowd, but regardless of whether or not they believe it was all made up, they cannot deny the fact that they were thoroughly entertained from start to finish.

FEARLESS

In show business, if you go up on stage and don't do well, it is referred to as "dying." According to the National Institute of Mental Health,[2] over two-thirds of the US population fear death. The only thing feared more by Americans is public speaking. So to get up on stage and entertain folk requires a level of fearlessness.

The most fearful game Colin and Brad play is a game called Kick It. In this game, the audience suggests a premise for

---

[2] Study verified 8/18/2012, 74% of the US population is afraid of public speaking (glossophobia), 68% is afraid of death (necrophbia)

the scene and Colin and Brad act it out. That's the easy part. Whenever Colin or Brad say something, the other can interject with the words "kick it," then rap music is played over the speakers and the lights start flashing to the beat. If Colin were to say this to Brad, Brad would have to start rapping about what he just said, coming up with a story that flows and rhymes, all while keeping it in tune. He has to keep it going until Colin is satisfied and says "word," cueing the end of the rap.

It is described as a mutual torture game and is the game Colin and Brad fear the most. Once the music starts, there's no turning back. They can't stop and start over. They are on an island completely exposed, and need to be fearless.

As difficult as that is, it's not this fearlessness that impresses me most about Colin and Brad.

Brad has told me that despite over ten years of touring with Colin, and many more in the future, he will never eclipse the number of free shows he has done by the number of paid shows he is doing. That was an impactful statement and is very telling. Despite improv being made up as you go, it takes a lot of work to be good at it. You have to put yourself out there and not be afraid to fail. It was Brad's thousands of performances at clubs where he tried things out, learned from his mistakes and wasn't afraid to be bad, that made him so good now.

Colin told me a story about a time early in his career when he was struggling in Los Angeles. He and his wife sat down with pencil and paper to make a list of their skills and see what other work they could do if the show business thing didn't work out. Colin said within five minutes his wife Debra was making a shopping list while he was drawing pictures. The point is, they didn't want to do anything else; they knew they needed to make show business work. They were afraid at the time because things were not going according to plan, but it was this fear that motivated them toward success.

parting thoughts

The secret to Colin and Brad's success is that they've always challenged themselves. In the beginning it was for survival. Now, with all of their success, it is to keep it fresh. You might think their motivation to keep it fresh is to provide the audience with a great show. I don't think that's their motivator. They have so much experience that they could mail in performances for the rest of their careers and the audiences would still be entertained and enjoy the shows. I believe their motivation is from within. They want to challenge themselves because they thrive on it. That makes the show fun for them and ultimately even better for the audience.

There are moments of fear every night when they are backed into a corner and need to get out of it by saying something witty and funny. They do not dodge that fear. They take it head on, and that's why they are successful.

chapter 6

How Did David Copperfield Make the Statue of Liberty Disappear?

exposed

When people learn I am a magician there are a few questions I commonly get. "Can you make [fill in the blank, usually a spouse] disappear?" or "Can you saw [again fill in the blank with a spouse] in half?" I have to politely smile and act as if it's the first time I ever heard that. They always think they are so clever when they say it, too. It makes me wonder how many things I say to a waitress or flight attendant that I think are clever and that they've heard a dozen times earlier that day. Probably a lot. It's in some people's nature and, I guess, I shouldn't complain because I, too, can be one of those people.

The questions that I can complain about are when they ask me how I am able to do something. Like, "How did you turn that $1 bill into a $100 bill?" They ask as if I am willing to tell them the secret. My theory on magic tricks is that they have two parts, the magic and the trick. The trick is fake, it is physically impossible to transform a $1 bill into a $100 bill, and if it were physically possible, no doubt it would be illegal. The magic part, however, is real. That sense of wonder we have when we see something amazing is magic. It is a real emotion.

If I were to explain the trick part, I would destroy the magic part. People think they want to know how a magic trick is done, but if they are told, they are almost always disappointed because they no longer have that sense of wonder. That is why I do not reveal the secrets of the "tricks" that I do.

This can be very frustrating to real inquisitive types. They feel that they are owed an explanation and can be quite persistent. When it becomes clear that they are not going to get a secret from me, they switch gears and ask me how some other magician does something, thinking, I suppose, that I will tell them.

The most frequently asked question is, "How did David Copperfield make the Statue of Liberty disappear?" This is an illusion that was performed decades ago but is arguably the most famous illusion of modern magic. To reveal how David did this would be unethical.

So, here is *how* David did it. Okay, I wrote *how* not because I'm going to reveal the "trick," but having spent time talking with David about his career, I think I know *how* he did it, *how* he was able to pull off the greatest illusion of our time and *how* he has become the most successful, by any measure, magician in history. The *how* I am going to explain is much more valuable then the *how* people think they want to hear.

If I had to summarize the secret to his success in one word, it would be passion. David's work ethic is legendary. He told me about his day, but let's start with his evening. He does two shows a night at the MGM Grand in Las Vegas. When the shows are over at 11:00 pm he does a variety of things from rehearsing a new routine on stage to giving a tour of his museum to catching a movie. He won't be home until at least 2:00 am and he'll be back at his museum and workshop busy with work by 8:00 am. He tries to make time for a nap before his shows but many times obligations prevent that, such as a third matinee show on Saturdays. Every Las Vegas show I can think of is dark a couple days of the week, not David. You can see his show twice a night any night and three times on Saturdays.

David works more than anyone I've ever met. He truly doesn't see it that way though. To him he is just passionate about his projects. It is still very much physically exhausting and how he is able to do it remains a mystery to me. When you are passionate about something it never feels like work.

As I say, his passion is his secret. It was his passion for the movies that led him to create themed vignettes for magic effects. These themed pieces separated him from other magicians at the time and made him more recognizable, just like Walt Disney creating a themed park distinguished from other entertainment parks at the time.

In describing his passion in an interview, David said that no one wakes up in the morning wondering if he can push a cigarette through a quarter (referencing a popular "standard" magic effect where a lit cigarette is pushed through the center of a quarter leaving the quarter intact after the cigarette goes all the way through). Done that way the effect is much more "trick" than "magic" and David didn't want to do standard effects that are more tricks than magic. He wanted to create a greater emotional response than the curiosity of how the "trick" was done. He wanted to elicit an emotional response to the story he was telling.

Hearing him say this had a profound affect on me. It became clear why he was different from the rest of the magicians out there, it became even more clear when I had an opportunity to ask him my own questions. I wanted to dig deeper into this topic, and I was glad I did.

David's passion is pure. It's not about being famous or having wealth, although those are the byproducts. It's about putting on the best performance out there. David claims he was lucky to find what separated him from others magicians. Many will disagree with him and say it was a result of his hard work, and there was nothing lucky about it.

While hard work certainly plays a huge part in David's success, I happen to agree with David, although I personally prefer the term "good fortune." David was fortunate that what he was most passionate about resonated so well with audiences. There are plenty of passionate people in the world, but few of them are estimated to be worth one billion dollars. The great thing about passion, though, is that it is independent of financial wealth.

While I did not ask David directly, I got the sense from him and from others, and have experienced myself, that when you are doing the thing you are most passionate about, the money doesn't matter. Sure, you need enough to survive, but you are not working for a paycheck, you are working for something much greater than that. On the flip side, it is very rare that you will find an uber successful person that is not passionate about their work.

You need to have that passion to persevere. Just because David was, and is, passionate about his work doesn't mean he's had an easy time of it. There were very difficult times in his early career. Most notably, when he finished a run as a teenager in *The Magic Man* that played in Chicago, he moved back to New York City and struggled. Opportunities were few and far between, so when given one, he took it. He didn't turn an opportunity down because he didn't think it was a fit for his longer term goals. He wasn't like the deadbeat relative, long unemployed, who is "holding out for a management position."[3] David took the opportunity and found a way to shape it and make it of value to his long term goals.

David wanted to do a television special, but he did not "hold out for a television special;" he kept knocking on

---

[3] I originally wanted to reference "Cousin Eddy" from *Christmas Vacation* but was told many people would not "get" the reference. I hope you do because I laugh every time I think of that scene.

doors. He received a lot of rejections but did not waver. That is not to say he was not discouraged, he was. But he persevered until he made it happen. With celebrities like David we generally only see their finished product. We don't see the countless hours spent selling the show, we don't see the countless hours put into refinement. We don't see all the ups and downs associated with the process.

Recounting all of David's success, I naively asked him if he ever has a lull in motivation, if he is ever discouraged now, in spite of his success. David replied by saying, "I am not a robot." He has lulls and relies on other people to help him, just like every other human being.

So *how* did David Copperfield make the Statue of Liberty vanish? He remained passionate about his craft. He separated himself from the pack and worked through adversity. These words, which seem so simple and are easy to write and say, are much more difficult to live. Passion is the beginning and end for David. It all began with passion, and if you are not passionate about your goals you won't distinguish yourself, you won't be motivated to work through the tough times. David is as passionate today as he was when he produced his first television special. Passion is the common thread we find in every successful person.

FEARLESS

David's new show, *Live the Impossible*, is very personal to him. It was inspired by the lessons taught to him by his father; how we need to embrace our fears and push through them. If fear is not there, we will lose our edge. David explained to me that to this day fear is his primary motivator. You would think after tens of thousands of performances, he wouldn't have any fear, he would be fearless.

It's definitely not stage fright, but he still has a fear of being a disappointment to his audience. This fear motivates him while his passion keeps him focused, allowing him to enjoy the process. As his father said to him, fear is not a bad thing, it is something to be embraced.

Fear has been a part of him throughout his career. Before doing his first television special he was afraid it would not go well. When it was highly successful and he was offered more television specials, the fear was still there. Would the next one still be good? It is good to have this fear...as long as you confront it.

parting thoughts

When I was younger I used to think, if I just had the money that David Copperfield had, I could do a television special. As I matured I realized that is not the case at all. Knowing David, it couldn't be more clear. They say success breeds success. I'm not sure who they are, but in this case I think they are right. If you gave an amateur magician all the financial resources to put together a television special on magic, I guarantee you it would be terrible. That amateur has not earned his or her success. It is through the achievement of that first success that future successes become more probable. They are not necessarily easier, just more probable. With that first success one knows better what it will take. David has great resources at his disposal, but with or without them, the process remains the same. Each new success takes passion and a willingness to push through fear, neither of which can be bought.

chapter 7

Does ESP Exist?

exposed

Have you ever had something happen that seemed so much more than a coincidence that you felt it had to be a sign of some kind, perhaps a sign of some cosmic force speaking to you? I'm sure you have; we all have. This may be difficult for you to accept, but…

It's just the law of probability!

If you disagree, please try to read the following with an open mind. Think of the day you had today. Throughout each day you have many experiences to which you pay little attention because, in one form or another, they are rather frequent and quite ordinary. However, when one of those ordinary experiences seems to be not so ordinary, we take notice. We feel like we need a better explanation than "this was just a coincidence." But it was just that. A coincidence. Really.

Throughout each day we have thousands of random experiences. Multiply those by the number of days you have lived and you have literally millions of them. The probability of one, or two, or a dozen of those experiences seeming supernatural is pretty good.

Some of you, perhaps many of you, will disregard this argument. You will continue to believe there are deeper meanings to some of your coincidental experiences. Some of you seek after such experiences. The fact is that the world is full of charlatans and con artists who use this predilection to make a living. Hopefully you have not fallen prey to them, but it is quite possible that you know someone who has!

Have you ever been to a séance? I have, and the first few times I attended with an open mind. I thought it would be interesting to have a supernatural experience and I accepted the medium at face value. A medium is a spiritualist who claims to communicate with the dead. But it became clear that belief in what he was saying required me to connect dots that had no business being connected. I watched others in the room connect the dots with excitement. They believed everything the medium said. They *wanted* to believe and they did.

In the early 1900s, Harry Houdini, a name you may recognize, felt driven to expose fake mediums who prey on people who desperately wanted to believe. Houdini actually hoped he would find a medium who could help him communicate with his late mother, but he never did, and he was appalled by the unethical behavior of those who take money from people by pretending to tell their future or, even worse, claiming to be able to relate a message from a deceased loved one. In Houdini's experience, every medium he ever met was a fake!

There is a big difference between a magician making a prediction for entertainment purposes and a fake medium falsely speaking on behalf of the deceased. When we watch a magician, we know it is a trick. If the magician could really predict the future, why would he waste his time doing magic? He would be playing the lottery! He would be hired by Las Vegas casinos to do their handicapping! We don't ask this question because we know it's a trick.

Despite the lack of scientific evidence that ESP does exist, many people still want to believe in it, and when the desire to believe is strong enough, it is very difficult to convince them otherwise.

Conflict between believers of the paranormal and skeptics have continued from Houdini's time to the present day. Most notably in recent times, James Randi championed the effort to debunk pseudoscience. In fact, he created a foundation that offered prize money, now at $1 million, for any person or persons able to prove they have paranormal abilities. After fifty years, and thousands of applicants, the prize money remains unclaimed.

The director of the James Randi Education Foundation is a man named Banachek, who was once declared by scientists to have psychic abilities. As a youth, Banachek participated in a four-year study conducted scientists by the Washington University (St. Louis) McDonnell Laboratory for Psychical Research (the MAC Lab). The study consisted of 160 hours of experiments run by scientists on people who supposedly possessed psychic abilities, from 1979 to 1981.

In a "controlled" environment, Banachek was able to bend spoons, stop clocks, and set fire to fuses with the power of his mind. I emphasize the word "controlled" because, as Banachek explained it to me, the scientists involved were persuaded that the test subjects needed a relaxed environment in order to summon their psychic powers. Therefore, conditions were relaxed and controls were often compromised. Scientists were very excited about the teenaged Banachek, and concluded that he did, in fact, have psychic abilities. Their experiments were flawed, however. It turned out that Banachek, a prodigy mentalist, was part of James Randi's secret Project Alpha, an elaborate hoax planted within the study.

When the McDonnell Laboratory for Psychical Research was established, James Randi, the recipient of a prestigious MacArthur Foundation Fellowship (often referred to as a "genius grant"), offered his services as a conjuror to help the research scientists detect chicanery. His offer was rejected. They were, after all, noted parapsychologists. Because of Randi's deep-seated belief that psychic powers are fake, he set out to prove it. He trained two young boys, one of them Banachek, in the ways of psychic trickery and encouraged them to apply as test subjects. The two boys were selected, and throughout the four years of experimentation succeeded in making those parapsychologists believe their powers were legitimate. The purpose was not to embarrass the scientists, but rather to emphasize that well-trained scientists are as susceptible to deception and self-deception as anyone else.

Banachek confided in me that an unforeseen consequence for him, one that he struggled with, was the realization that those scientists were good people striving for truth, and some of them were going to be embarrassed or hurt. After all, they were human beings with human passions and desires. At times the desire to believe can cloud reason and weave partial truths into suppositions that convince our hearts that what is, is not, and what is not, is. Banachek shared an example of this. Parapsychologists have long believed that under certain conditions the camera can catch the presence of spirits. Sir Arthur Conan Doyle, the creator of Sherlock Holmes, was convinced he had photographs that proved the existence of fairies. When Banachek was asked if he could photograph spirits he said, "Yes!" At that moment he hadn't a clue as to how he would do it. Mind you, this was before Photoshop and digital cameras. The camera given him used film! Banachek was to take the picture and give the camera to a parapsychologist, who would remove the film, develop it, and print the photo. This was done. And there in the photo was a vague, rather nebulous white shape. Clear evidence of a ghost! How was it done? Just before Banachek took his photo he simply spat on the camera lens. The "saliva filter" altered the image enough for people's imaginations to get the best of them, and they were sure they were seeing the supernatural. They wanted to believe, and they did!

Belief ran so deep that when they were told of the Project Alpha hoax the parapsychologists refused to believe it. They argued that if Banachek was capable of lying to them, who was to say that the lie was not from Randi about the hoax in general. Maybe Banachek really did have psychic powers and maybe Randi convinced him to lie and say it was a hoax!

Banachek, an unknown teenager at the time, was able to use techniques developed by magicians and mentalists, many of them his own, to fool the scientists. Today he is a hugely successful psychic entertainer, known to the public as someone who accomplishes the impossible, and to the magic and mentalism community for his skill and ingenuity. He has authored books on the subject of psychic entertainment and has created effects used by many of today's top magicians. In addition, he is a consultant in many fields outside of the magic community.

I first encountered Banachek when a friend of mine was producing a show called *Conned*. The show, as the title suggests, featured several varieties of con artists. A con is a way to defraud one or more people for the purpose of monetary gain. A con *artist* is a person especially adept ad doing this. The show featured a pickpocket, a card cheat, and a mental manipulator. Based on Banachek's reputation, I recommended him to my friend for the show. At the time I had never met him, but over the course of developing the show and its first couple of runs, I had the pleasure of getting to know Banachek well.

For Banachek's part in *Conned*, he did several demonstrations of what he calls "thought manipulation." His approach was different from that of a mentalist or a magician. For example, in one particular presentation he began by showing a sealed envelope that he labeled "proof." A magician or mentalist would call it a prediction, but Banachek explained that he was not about to predict the future, but rather influence choices the audiences would make, and that the contents of the envelope would prove just that.

Banachek went through a series of questions directed at random people in the audience, each time using a different technique to lead them to choose his desired outcome. He would ask a question and, after receiving an answer, he would ask, "Do you think that was a free choice?" The audience has no reason to believe otherwise, so the participant replied, "Yes." "It was not a free choice!" said Banachek. He then explained the method he used to influence the person making the choice. The audience responded with a collective, "Ahhh."

After repeating this several times, Banachek's customary follow up question, "Do you think that was a free choice?" was no longer answered with a "Yes." The audience was not exactly sure how the choice was influenced, but they knew they were about to find out.

At the end of these entertaining questions and explanations, Banachek turned to the envelope containing the "Proof." When the envelope was opened, the contents were revealed to match the responses of the audience. There was no longer any room for doubt; Banachek had influenced the choices. Still, there are always some who think they are seeing real psychic phenomena. It's human nature.

Banachek presents everything in an entertaining way and makes clear that his presentations are for entertainment purposes, nothing more. One of Banachek's most entertaining routines has to do with fork bending. While he holds a dinner fork, the handle seems to visibly bend by the force of his mind alone. The tines twist in impossible directions, and some of this happens in the hands of a spectator! While Banachek explains to his audiences how he is able to manipulate their thoughts, he bends forks as a trick, without explanation, to highlight how convincing such presentations can be. Some magic effects are so convincing, they leave people believing they are real, even when the performer says they are not. Fork bending is like that. Banachek tells his audience he has no supernatural powers, yet there are still people who believe he has psychic abilities despite his denial.

This is nothing new. Nearly one hundred years ago, Houdini, in his crusade to expose mediums by duplicating their "psychic tricks" as entertainment in order to prove the absence of supernatural happenings, had a friend who could not be convinced they were tricks. This was none other than Sir Arthur Conan Doyle, mentioned earlier, the creator of Sherlock Holmes, who was a master of deductive reasoning. Doyle, himself, was educated as a doctor. He never ceased to believe in supernatural sciences and abilities, supported spiritualistic mediums even when they had been proved fraudulent, and even believed Houdini achieved some of his famous escapes by the use of supernatural powers. This eventually put a strain on their friendship, which became quite contentious.

The power of belief is an incredible force, which when channeled in a positive direction, can accomplish amazing things.

FEARLESS

The advantage magicians or mentalists have over an audience is that they set the conditions for the show. They are in control. Banachek participated in project Alpha with the objective of fooling the team of MAC Lab scientists. That would put fear into the heart of the most seasoned magician, yet Banachek, while only a teenager, stepped into situations where he appeared to have given up total control, turning it over to the scientists and their test conditions.

That would ramp up fear for most of us exponentially! Not knowing what the conditions would be, Banachek could not plan for them. His challenge was always to adapt the techniques and skills he had mastered to the circumstances. The key to this was usually to persuade the scientists, through subtlety and suggestion, that the controls be modified in ways thought unimportant by the scientists, but which would return the advantage to Banachek. Still fear? Of course. What if he still lacked sufficient control?

You will recall that fear is related to knowledge and experience. Having both will reduce fear and allow one to confront it. Having one without the other heightens fear. In most cases we have the knowledge and not the experience. In Banachek's case, he had the experience of performing psychic effects and had considerable knowledge of how people respond on such occasions, but he did not have knowledge of the test conditions. He had limited knowledge, but considerable experience.

Did he ever consider that he would fail, be found out? I don't know for sure. I would have been afraid that would happen. The point is that Banachek forced himself to confront his circumstances. Once he entered the examination room there was no turning back. He had one simple rule that got him through — never panic. Regardless of the request and conditions presented to him, he would never panic. He realized that a true psychic would not necessarily be correct every time. Therefore, Banachek was not afraid to fail at the test at first. Then, with the experience gained, he would come up with ways to apply his knowledge, a little here, then a little more, until he once again had proved, to the accepting minds of the scientists, who wanted Banachek to be psychic, remember, that he was a true psychic. While he never knew what the scientists were going to ask of him, he did know his response would be "Sure, I can do that." He never refused a challenge, or said it couldn't be done, and the rest is history. Amazing things can be accomplished when you force yourself to confront your fears.

parting thoughts

Psychic phenomena and so-called psychics are still very controversial topics. The general consensus is that the ability to use psychic powers to move or bend objects, or make predictions, does not exist. The subject of spiritualism, communication with the dead, is more complex. The fact is that there are many popular psychic entertainers who play to packed audiences by claiming what they do is real. Many people would like to communicate with their deceased loved ones and want to believe it is possible. I have very close friends myself, whom I respect and care for, who believe it is possible. Entertainers, indeed! Con Man is not synonymous with entertainer!

When a mentalist successfully makes a prediction, we are compelled to ask, "why not play the lottery?" Why don't spiritualist mediums contact Washington, Jefferson and Lincoln for advice? Why aren't they contacting religious figures from the past? I'm afraid I just can't believe.

But when people have strong beliefs, often no amount of evidence can convince them to the contrary. In itself, that is not a bad thing, if you have carefully considered your beliefs. We have used paranormal powers in this chapter as the means for addressing the power of belief and the dangers of wishful thinking, even blind faith. Hopefully Banachek's experiences have convinced you that blind faith is suspect. My objective in this chapter is not to convince you one way or another about ESP. I am clear where I stand,

and you should consider the alternatives. The primary objective, however, is to emphasize the power of belief. There is a difference in believing in psychic powers and believing in yourself! Never give up on believing in yourself. Never doubt that you can overcome your fears.

What should you take away from this chapter? First, Banachek has proved many times over, with his work at the MAC Labs 35 years ago, and through his work in the years that have followed, that most so-called psychic phenomena can be duplicated by the skills and methods of conjuring, enough to caution us about all so-called psychic phenomena. Therefore, approach belief with caution. Second, Banachek's experiences with the MAC Labs provide a perfect example of how fear can be overcome by applying the formula: fear + experience (enhanced by knowledge) = success. In his case his training for paranormal testing and his own extraordinary abilities to adapt and invent new ways to meet those tests enabled him to turn the negative energy often associated with fear into positive energy, leading him to the desired outcome. And finally, Banachek's key to controlling fear is one that we should apply to all aspects of our lives: when confronted by difficulties, off stage and on — don't panic. Sage advice.

chapter 8

You Won't See This Coming

exposed

The world of magic and magicians includes many genres, including mentalism, hypnotism, the art of the pick pocket, and juggling, to name a few. One that fascinates me the most is cheating at cards, sometimes called sharping. A card cheat uses the exact same techniques as a card magician, but for very different purposes.

Most card cheats, for obvious reasons, keep a low profile. The ones we are aware of use their skills for entertainment purposes, and are not really cheats. They are called card experts. While they easily, and frequently, perform card tricks, they more often showcase their skills in the form of gambling demonstrations. Perhaps it is because cheating at cards represents the dark side of card magic that the genre is so fascinating to me. Card cheating is illegal and dangerous - heavy, tough - so when the skills of the card cheat are presented for entertainment purposes, it feels like a demonstration of raw skill.

In a card cheating demonstration, the card cheat shows us exactly what he or she is doing, often in slow-motion. In real-time speed we don't see the "work" as it is called, but we know it happened when the cards are shown. There is no mystery of what happened, the "work," has been explained, but there is still very much a sense of wonder in *how* it was done. Watching a card cheat work is not unlike watching a juggler, in the sense that both are displays of skills requiring thousands of hours of practice.

A card cheat will tell the audience he is controlling a card from the middle of the pack to the top because he needs the card for his hand. A magician will use the same sleight-of-hand technique to move a spectator's selected card from the middle of the pack to the top because he needs it to magically appear. Watching the card cheat, the audience marvels at his or her skill. Watching the magician, the audience may say, "Oh, the card was just controlled to the top."

The skill of a magician is seldom fully appreciated. If a move requiring skill is done well, it should be invisible to the audience and appear as if nothing happened. A card cheat's move is still invisible to the audience, but the audience is aware that something has happened and appreciates the skill required to make it happen.

Richard Turner is considered by many to be the greatest card cheat of our time. That title was awarded to him by the late Dai Vernon, aptly referred to as "the professor," who was the most sought after teacher of magic in the 20th Century. Cards and card cheating was of supreme interest to Vernon, who had seen all of the magicians and many of the underground cheats in his nearly one hundred years of life, from 1894 to 1992. Even more than 20 years after Vernon's death his evaluation of Richard Turner carries considerable weight.

How did Richard become the world's greatest card mechanic? The same way you get to Carnegie Hall: practice, practice, practice. I am not talking about a few hours a day. Sure you can become very good with that kind of effort, but not even close to Richard. For many years Richard Turner practiced 10 hours or more a day, everyday.

That may seem impossible, but having spent time with Richard I accept it as fact. Richard has a deck of cards with him at all times. He also carries a small felt board that he uses as a lap table. If you engage him in a conversation he will shuffle cards non stop. These aren't ordinary shuffles, he's controlling cards the whole time. This means he is moving cards up and down through the deck and knows where every card in the deck is located at all times. This requires intricate sleight-of-hand which he executes with the greatest of ease. It is simply muscle memory for him.

The first time I met Richard it was at a meeting for officers of The Society of American Magicians. Richard performed for us earlier in the day and amazed everyone. I was literally inches from his hands. He explained what he was doing and yet I couldn't see a thing. Later that evening at a stage show I happened to sit in front of Richard. I knew he was behind me because I could hear the riffling of cards as he continued to practice.

It is safe to say the man is obsessed. He has no problem recognizing that. It is his nature and it extends beyond cards. When traveling, the first thing he asks when checking in to a new hotel is, "Where's the gym?" Richard, will work out two or more hours everyday while on the road. And, of course, these are not ordinary workouts. The only way I can describe them is to say they are insane. Richard does not see them that way, as he alternates sets of one hundred push ups and one hundred sit ups several times in ten minutes before going on to other inconceivable repetitions of cardio and weight training activities.

He has been obsessed with physical fitness since he began studying martial arts at the age of 17, and he has a 5th degree black belt in Wado Kai karate. If you're as lucky to spend time with him, as I have been, you'll hear incredible stories from a showdown with Chuck Norris to a fight with a shark. Yes, Richard is insane, but in the best possible way. Let me share with you some of my personal stories from my time traveling with him.

While traveling between cities for shows, at times Richard would take a break from his practicing to consult with the U.S. Playing Card Company. This is the Ohio-based company that makes the popular Bicycle and Bee brand playing cards, as well as many other private label cards. In this particular case, Richard was sent a package containing two dozen decks of cards.

One dozen of the decks were labeled "1" through "12." The other dozen decks were labeled "A" through "L." Richard handled each deck, shuffling them to feel them out. He would then dictate notes to his son, Asa Spades Turner (really), who liked to travel with his dad. After a thorough evaluation of all the decks, he would call his contact at U.S. Playing Card Company (USPC).

The conversation would start with some pleasantries and then get down to business. The first order of business was for Richard to tell which numbered decks matched which lettered decks. USPC had sent Richard decks of cards with various card laminates, stock, thickness, coatings, cuts and other processes. They sent two decks of each variety, one labeled with a letter, the other labeled with a number.

If Richard correctly told them which lettered decks match the numbered decks, they knew Richard was on his game and that his evaluations would have merit. It was essentially a control. Richard was doing all of this evaluation by his sense of touch. Once it was established that Richard's sense of touch was on point, he began his evaluation.

Very, very few people can tell a difference between the feel of Bicycle and Bee cards. To Richard, they are miles apart. He would comment about the thickness of a card, whether it was a single card stock or a laminate. He commented on the coating used on a card, and even the direction in which it was cut.

These are all important qualities to people who handle cards frequently such as casino dealers and professional gamblers. USPC needs to ensure that their cards meet quality standards as they constantly work to improve the manufacturing process. Richard is an invaluable resource to them. If a new card can match Richard's standard, there is little doubt anyone else will object.

How did Richard's sense of touch become so refined?

Obviously, it was through his countless hours of practice. Richard estimated that in the 10 day run of the show *Conned* he performed or practiced 720,000 card moves. This is more than most magicians will do in a lifetime. But the really interesting thing about Richard Turner is that he has accomplished all of these things in his life despite having lost his vision at an early age.

After recovering from scarlet fever at the age of nine, Richard's vision began to deteriorate. By the time he was fourteen, his eyesight was twice the limit of what was considered legally blind.

FEARLESS

Richard never uses the word blind and refuses to consider that he is handicapped. His vision is just another challenge in life. The fact is that Richard has more determination than anyone I have ever met. If there was ever a truly fearless man, it would be Richard. It doesn't take him but a second to accept a challenge and begin to work relentlessly to meeting it.

At some point in his life Richard put aside fear, and has faced every situation life has provided. Remember, it is not that he does not feel fear, he simply met it face on and set it aside. He simply refuses to acknowledge it. From my experiences with Richard, I believe that he is one of those unique individuals who has a high threshold for fear.

parting thoughts

I really don't know what I would do if I was dealt the hand Richard was dealt. I'd like to think I would view it like Richard does, as a challenge, and push right through it. If Richard ever feels depressed or sorry for himself, he keeps those emotions hidden. He is always upbeat, happy and ready to joke around and have fun.

Richard is also a very proud man and has many, many reasons to be so. He is also one of the most generous people I know. As quick as he is to take on a challenge, he is that quick to give a friend a hand. A documentary is being made about his life, the title of which is *Dealt*,[4] a perfect title for a man dealt what many would consider a difficult hand. Just like he does at the card table, Richard is able to turn any cards dealt to him into a winning hand.

---

[4] Information about the documentary on Richard's life, *Dealt*, can be found at dealtmovie.com

chapter 9

Are Sideshow Performers Really Doing that Stuff?

exposed

I've had an interest in magic for as long as I can remember, although it wasn't until my twelfth birthday that I started seriously practicing the art. I was spending my summer vacation in San Diego, and while walking around Seaport Village, a series of shops by the water, I discovered my first magic shop.

The shop was going out of business, and everything was half off. I also had birthday money burning a hole in my pocket. It was a perfect storm, and I was hooked. I bought as many props and gimmicks as my birthday money would allow. It was not long before I considered myself an expert in the field – not unlike my confidence in my writing skills at the time!

One of my most prized possessions was an amazing deck of cards called the Svengali Deck, which enabled me to do many amazing things. I quickly learned to perform three or four tricks and was confident that I was now the Master of the Svengali!

A few weeks later I was at the Corvette Diner, watching the resident magician, Magic Mike Stillwell, who stopped at our table.

"Would you like to see some magic?" he asked.

"Sure!" I replied with enthusiasm.

Magic Mike pulled out a deck of cards. I smiled. After all, I was Master of the Svengali. I had actually never seen a magician perform close-up magic with cards before and I was blown away by what Magic Mike did that day. Those card tricks were just not possible with my Svengali Deck. Maybe there were other kinds of trick decks. I had to find out what kind of deck he was using. I *needed* to get a deck like that!

When Magic Mike took a performance break, I found my way to where he was relaxing.

"Excuse me," I said with a smile. "You are really a great magician. I am a magician too. My name is Vinny, Vinny Grosso. I was wondering what kind of trick deck you were using for those card tricks."

He smiled at me. "Bicycle," he said.

"Bicycle?"

"Yep."

"Those are just regular cards, the kind my relatives use to play Gin Rummy. Bicycle?"

"Yep."

I didn't understand. Bicycle "rider back" playing cards really are just regular cards you can buy at any grocery or drug store. The backs have a swirly design that includes cartoon drawings of little angels riding bicycles with an airplane propeller in the center. There are no gimmicks or special doodads that would help me accomplish the impossible. As this sunk in, I looked at Magic Mike in puzzlement and said the only thing that came to mind: "But, how?"

Mike said, "The Royal Road to Card Magic."

He was a master of the short answer. It turned out that *The Royal Road to Card Magic* is the title of a classic book on card magic that can be found in almost every magician's library. Magic Mike did go on to explain that he accomplished his "miracles" with sleight-of-hand he had learned from the book, *The Royal Road to Card Magic*. He told me I could learn them, too, and that was the day I discovered a whole new world of magic that is accomplished by hard work, practice, and skill, rather than just gimmicks and doodads.

That discovery was reinforced several years later as I watched a variety of performers at a unique restaurant in New York City called "Mostly Magic," which, sadly, closed after a long and successful life. The emcee, Todd Robbins, startled me by eating a light bulb. Later he hammered a four-inch nail into his left nostril. For his finale, he inflated a rubber water bottle until it burst by blowing into it like blowing up a balloon! Was this magic? He certainly created wonder and awe! Was he using trick light bulbs, nails and water bottles? Surely he was!

For some odd reason I became obsessed with his work. How was he able to hammer that nail into his nose? Where could I get a collapsible nail? How did he switch the trick nail for the real one he passed out at the end, although not many people wanted to touch it! Did I want to hammer a nail into my nose? Naaah! … Probably not.

It wasn't until years later that I discovered they weren't tricks at all. Todd Robbins really did hammer a nail into his nose; he really did eat a light bulb! Cool! Gross, but Cool! And, yes, about the time I discovered those things I, too, decided to learn how to hammer a nail into my nose.

The effect is called "block head," in sideshow parlance, and is one of the most common stunts in that unique genre of magic. They are called "stunts" because, almost always, the performers are doing exactly what they appear to be doing. No trickery. I now speak with authority, because after a reasonable period of practice, more conditioning, really, and gradually gaining more and more nerve, I was able to do just that – hammer a four-inch nail all the way into my nose, and it is frequently a part of my performances.

This is, by far, my mother's least favorite thing I do, and I am pretty sure if I weren't into magic, I would not like to see it either. However, for some bizarre reason, I absolutely love to perform it. But mastering "block head" was only the beginning. I became hooked on sideshow stunts.

After "block head," I learned how to eat fire. After fire eating, I learned how to put my bare hand into an animal trap. And after the animal trap, I learned the mystery of swallowing razor blades. There wasn't a disgusting or gory stunt that I did not want to learn, which is odd, because I am easily grossed out!

The most recent stunt added to my repertoire is walking barefoot on broken glass. I had seen this presented several different ways, but none more effectively than that performed by Doc Swan. Doc Swan is a master at sideshow stunts who has done virtually every side show stunt in the book. But his approach makes him unique. There is nothing funny about sticking fishhooks through the fleshy pockets under the eyes, or dancing on broken shards of beer and wine bottles with bare feet, but when Doc does this it is hilarious. That is, *he* is hilarious. He is a comedian who uses sideshow stunts for his medium, and regardless of the danger, or apparent gore, his audiences convulse in laughter as they join Doc in a side-splitting comedy adventure. This is kind of odd, in a way, because they are cringing in horror at the same time.

Doc Swan performs for a living; it's his profession, and his specialty is doing sideshow stunts. What he does he learned on his own. He didn't read it out of a book and he never took lessons. He watched other sideshow performers do their stunts and then figured out a way to do the same thing, only better if possible, and then make people laugh. This is a dangerous way to learn dangerous stunts, and it is a wonder Doc did not hurt himself. But that is how Doc did it, and like most artistic masters, he holds his secrets dear. In fact, Doc has only shared his secrets with two people.

In the seventies he taught a young Penn Jillette, of Penn & Teller fame, his techniques for eating fire. Then, in 2013, he taught me his techniques for walking on broken glass. But Doc didn't agree to share his secrets right away. He knew I was interested in learning, but before he felt comfortable teaching me we spent considerable time talking about magic and the sideshow. He was testing just how committed and serious I really was. He knew I performed frequently, he knew I had been National President of The Society of

American Magicians, but he wasn't sure I had the passion for sideshow stunts. To my delight, he agreed.

Glass walking is dangerous. Many people think that the broken glass is just large chunks of dull glass, but this is not the case. The broken glass includes razor-sharp edges, knife-like shards, and tiny splinters that are extremely painful when embedded in the skin. Doc described to me many of his most painful cuts and splinters, most of which did not actually occur during a performance. They occurred either in the preparation for or the clean up after a performance. I was almost deterred when he explained that the tiny shards, or splinters, become completely embedded under the skin and the slightest touch causes severe pain. Removing them is extremely difficult, as they tend to slide in more deeply with the effort to get them out. Was I afraid? I'll get to that.

I did learn, and Doc has followed up every so often to see how I am doing. With every call Doc asked if I had developed a routine yet. The stunt was basic, he had told me, but it is nothing without a routine, which is necessary for an entertaining performance. "Work on the routine, Vinny," Doc said again and again. That was the real challenge.

I told Doc that I wanted to do something different. Because the focus of my performances is on overcoming fear, I wanted to bring someone from the audience to the stage and have that person join me in walking barefoot across the bed of glass. It would be a strong, visual demonstration of overcoming fear. Doc's initial reaction was not positive. He was concerned that if I taught someone to walk on glass in two minutes, on stage, in front of the audience, how could I expect that audience to be impressed that I could walk on glass? It was a great question, and something I hadn't thought about.

I had other suggestions, and he had other questions. I do have a routine now, in large part because Doc Swan saw in me a passion to help others overcome their fears and understood that I could use sideshow stunts to help me toward that goal. My presentation allows for an audience member to overcome their fear and take a step on the glass while still conveying the very real danger and skill required to do a full glass walk.

FEARLESS

As I have explained, Doc is self taught. I had heard about musicians and painters being self taught, but never considered how sideshow performers learn their stunts. But, after all, there is not much danger of physical pain in learning to play a musical instrument or paint a picture, but almost every sideshow stunt can cause injury. They are exactly what they appear to be. There is no trick to them. The secret is that you have to set aside fear, and trust that you can do it. Could I have learned the stunts I use by myself? Perhaps, but I was extremely fortunate to have Todd Robbins, Doc Swan, and others help me to overcome fear.

I tried to learn to eat fire by myself. Before I ever struck a match, I found books on fire eating and read them carefully. I found instructions on how to make torches, what kind of fuel to use, and how to extinguish the torch in my mouth. I did not find instructions for putting my fear aside. I had good knowledge, although limited, but I had no experience in eating fire. As a result, I simply could not find the courage to make a torch and try it on my own. I was too afraid.

I determined that I needed someone to lead me through it, like Doc had done with my glass walking. I was fortunate to find an expert fire eater to show me, to lead me through it. In this case his experience compensated for my lack of experience. He helped me put my fear aside, and I learned that there is more than one way to become fearless.

parting thoughts

Doc Swan is one of the purest performers I know. He eats, sleeps and breathes performing. He has more material than he'll ever need, yet he continues to develop new stunts and tweak and refine old stunts. He is not afraid to toss out a stunt that he feels does not quite work, even if he as spent years developing the skill and presentation of that routine. If it doesn't fit, it doesn't fit. Now this may seem odd, but tossing out a favorite routine requires a kind of fearless behavior. It is kind of like sending off your first-born to college. You are afraid to see him or her go out into the cruel world, but you know it is for the best. You gather courage and put your fear behind you and send them off.

If a routine is not funny, even though Doc may love the stunt, the routine goes. If my stunt cannot emphasize the message that forms the nucleus of my show, it goes.

chapter 10

Unexplainably Amazing and Fearless

exposed

How good is your memory? When you are introduced to someone, can you recall their name two minutes later? Five minutes? A week later? When someone tells you a phone number, can you recall it or do you have to write it down? I have a terrible memory and it feels like it has only worsened since I gave up caffeine nearly ten years ago!

I cannot, for the life of me, remember a phone number. A person's name? Forget about it. It bothers me that I can't do this and it fascinates me how others can. I am amazed that actors can memorize their lines. When I perform, I struggle to recite scripted lines. Memory just doesn't come naturally to me, and I don't think I am alone.

My nephew Jesse learned to read at the age of three, and by the time he was five, I'm pretty sure he had surpassed my own reading level! He also has an amazing memory. We first noticed this when he was around four years old. I made a family calendar filled with pictures of my parents, siblings, their spouses and children, and marked it with everyone's birth dates. Jesse enjoyed looking through the calendar and, to our surprise, memorized it! He began to ask questions

like, "Do you know when Uncle Mike's birthday is?" Before
we were able to reply he would quip, "It's December 13th."
He knew everyone's birthday and began inquiring about the
years in which they were born. He then moved on to distant
relatives. I wouldn't be surprised if he knows *your* birthday!
He is our family's child prodigy.

This combination of learning to read very early, and
possessing an amazing memory has proved to be a powerful
combination. Jesse's thirst for reading and his ability to
memorize meant he would recall and recite anything he
read. Actually, this is not quite true. He does not have a
photographic memory. He just remembers things that
interest him. Like instruction sheets. Jesse would read the
instructions for board games and could recite them
verbatim, whether we needed them recited or not. When he
did this he did not change his tone, inflection, or cadence. It
was like listening to a "Speak-N-Spell," that early electronic
toy produced in the 1980s. It had a robotic, monotone voice
that would say a word. We had to spell it on a keyboard. If
we were right, the device replied, with an unenthusiastic,
"You are correct." That is how Jesse recited things.

I never liked "Speak-N-Spells" because, as I have said, I was and am a terrible speller. It was fun, however, to make it say inappropriate things, because it would say whatever letters we typed. Those words I could spell!

Fortunately, as Jesse has grown older (he is a ten–year-old at the time of this writing), he has made an effort to incorporate emotions and feelings into his speech. He now gets excited at just the right moments, is stern when it is called for, and can be quite entertaining. He even does celebrity impersonations!

Jesse loves movies and has applied his unique memory to them in amazing ways. He memorized details about the movies he sees by going on line and reading about them. He remembers a wide range of information. When asked about a movie, he can give us the date the movie was released, the production company or companies involved, and details about the logo variation used on screen before the credits are given. For a while Jesse was obsessed with logo variations, and took delight in telling us when the MGM Lion roared like the King of Beasts or mewed like a kitten. These variations are surprisingly popular with movie buffs, and several websites are devoted to them. We know this because Jesse found them and studied them. He is our living, breathing IMDB.[5] Do you have a question about a movie? Ask Jesse. It will be faster than looking up the answer on the internet!

I'm sure that you can tell from what I have written that Jesse is special. He has been diagnosed with Asperger's, which is an autism spectrum disorder, characterized by significant difficulties in social interaction and nonverbal communication, as well as restricted and repetitive patterns of behavior and interests. As you would expect, with the amazing ability to read and understand and memorize come other traits that range from cute to trying, for both Jesse and his family. As the case with many people with Asperger's, Jesse needs routine, his life to follow a certain order. With disarray, Jesse becomes anxious and agitated, and no amount of explanation or reasoning will help. For example, Jesse is very particular about what he eats and when he eats. Most foods must be prepared in a specific way or he simply won't eat them. His parents have learned to develop strategies for helping him to cope with change. An

---

[5] Internet Movie Data Base, imdb.com is a source for information about movies, from production information to the plot, most details about a particular movie or television show can be found there.

excellent example of this is the plan they follow in helping Jesse and the rest of the family plan for a family trip abroad.

Recognizing that cultural customs and differences, including eating times and popular foods, pose the possibility of real problems for Jesse, his parents have begun to help Jesse study about the countries they intend to visit. Fortunately, Jesse is also studying about these countries in school, which reinforces the interest expressed at home. As Jesse has been reading about the countries, he has been encouraged to memorize the popular foods of each country, how they are prepared, and when the meals are generally served. As a "fun" project, they are experimenting with those foods, and other cultural customs, in the comfort of their own home; that is, well before the trip. The plan is to eventually expand the "experiment" to ethnic restaurants.

While people with Asperger's dislike change and disorder, they actually do very well with rules. Rules represent consistency. Jesse's parents have discussed circumstances they are likely to face in foreign countries and have established rules that will need to be followed on the journey. They apply those rules to the experiment at home, as well. Jesse likes rules. He may not like or agree with all of them, but in his mind rules are to be followed, and he feels uncomfortable when there are none. Boundaries serve him well.

These trip rules, as well as other family rules, have been written down. Jesse loves to read, and remembers what he reads if it relates to his interests. Family rules are important to him because he is a part of the family. Trip rules are important to him because he will be a part of the family as they make the trip. It will be his trip, too.

Although they may be obsessed with something for a time, people with Asperger's do move on from one interest to another. Jesse's passion for movies and television has expanded to the world of YouTube and on-line videos. Jesse is currently making his own videos and has established a YouTube channel. He has created such enticing features as "Randomly Eating Chips," a video which, by his own admission, can be boring at times! However, his latest masterpiece is his creation of an episode of the Food Network television show, *Chopped*.

Jesse wrote the script, casted the show with cousins, aunts, uncles and grandparents, and directed and starred as the host. It was great fun until the first person got "chopped." Then typical family drama ensued, which was all caught on tape. It was a brilliant production by the young filmmaker!

FEARLESS

Jesse reacts to things in a unique way. Something as simple as a slice of pizza cut in a square instead of a triangle can be devastating to him. He is a sponge when it comes to gathering information, which he does when he finds an interest. He will learn and retain in his database even the smallest details about that topic. This represents knowledge, of course. But, perhaps because of his Asperger's, Jesse processes experiences differently from the rest of us. He seems to identify with the experience of other people, real or fictional, as though the experience is his own. By combining his knowledge with the vicarious experience, and if the experience he has observed has been positive, Jesse is never afraid to try it himself, and is likely to do quite well. However, if he is confronted by a variation of the experience, Jesse will have difficulty; he will be agitated. "This is not the way it is supposed to be!"

One evening, a few years ago, Jesse's mother found him hiding behind a curtain in his bedroom. He was afraid, and the fear lasted several days. It took some coaxing to get Jesse to share his anxiety, but he finally told his mother that he had read about haunted houses and monsters in a Halloween comic book. For the first time, Jesse learned about scary monsters. At the same time he processed the experience of the hero of the comic book as his own. It was a fictional experience, but it was real to Jesse. The result was debilitating fear.

In time, his mother was able to convince Jesse that the things he had read about were not real and couldn't possibly happen. It was not until Jesse acknowledged this internally that he was able to discredit his perceived "experience," and to dismiss the fear. The dynamics were very similar to my learning to eat fire. I needed someone to show me the way.

parting thoughts

Jesse's memory is absolutely amazing, but it is not photographic, for he only remembers information that is important to him. He doesn't hesitate to say, "I don't know," if you ask him about something in which he is not interested. He is not embarrassed about not knowing those things. We can't match Jesse's ability to remember whatever he wishes to, but there are tricks and techniques we can use to improve our memories.

One such technique is the memory peg system. This involves the creation of visual representations of what we want to remember. Most of us have difficulty remembering some of the ordinary things that happen to us, yet we retain memories of special occasions. Why? We were engaged mentally at those times and we usually can draw forward a mental picture of something from that occasion. We effectively incorporate a memory peg system without even knowing it.

The utilization of "memory pegs" can allow you to recall information you never would think possible. So what the heck is a memory peg? Well memory pegs require a little bit of memorization but not a lot, they're simpler then the multiplication tables you had to learn in elementary school. You can make memory pegs for as many numbers as you'd like but for this demonstration we'll use just ten.

So the memory peg is just an object associated with a number that is easy to recall. Our examples will be objects that rhyme or at least sound similar to the numbers. Here's the list:

1.   gun
2.   shoe
3.   tree
4.   door
5.   hive
6.   sticks
7.   heaven
8.   bait
9.   wine
10.   den

These objects associated with these numbers need to be committed to memory. It shouldn't take long because they sound so similar to the number.

Now the fun part, to memorize obscure things you create an image in your head and associate it with a memory peg. For example, if one of the things you are trying to remember is a burnt marshmallow, imagine a gun firing burnt marshmallows into the sky. The more vivid the image, the more effective the memory peg system is. I wouldn't imagine just any gun, but maybe a gatling gun, with a long flowing magazine of marshmallows and once they are fired they become burnt and charred. A burnt marshmallow will be forever associated in your mind with a gun and a gun is associated with the number one.

You can do this for as many items as you have memory pegs for. Try it with the list of ten I described earlier and then quiz yourself. You'll be amazed that no matter what number is asked for, the object comes right into your mind. It works the opposite way too; you can be told an object and you'll instantly be able to tell what number it is on your list.

chapter 11

Fooled Ya

tasteless

A magician wearing a tuxedo steps onto a stage with a Victorian backdrop. The audience, expecting a classy, sophisticated presentation of legerdemain, gets their first hint that they might be in for something different by the magician's opening line: "A magician wearing a tuxedo. How many of you sense something cheesy is about to go down?" The magician proceeds to explain that is more like a perception than a sense. A sense, he says, is like… sense of taste. And by the way, he continues, he is a picky eater, which he blames on having an *incredible sense of taste*.

By this time the audience is smiling. It's clear that this magician, although dressed for a stuffy, formal event, is far from stuffy. He's rather flip. Where could this be going? But that is just the beginning of his facetiousness, for he continues to explain that he will prove his incredible sense of taste in the only way a magician knows how, with a deck of cards. He also needs a volunteer, and after explaining that choosing a volunteer is a very delicate task, and how important it is to find someone with the right temperament, someone who will not upstage him, the magician introduces the comedian Carrot Top as his volunteer.

Carrot Top inspects the cards with some humorous byplay, and then the magician takes him through a series of inspections to eliminate any "sneaky stuff," explaining that some people believe that the magic he will perform is accomplished by means of electronic signaling. So Carrot Top is given a small flashlight to inspect the magician's ears, making sure there are no listening devices hidden within. Carrot Top confirms this. The magician states that he could be "wearing a wire," elaborating to explain such a device. "However, I assure you I am not wired," he says. No one appears to be convinced. Noticing this, the magician rips off his tuxedo, leaving him wearing just a Las Vegas Chippendales outfit: bowtie, white cuffs and black shorts.

The audience is both mildly shocked and amused, but as the magician points out, it is clear they are still not entirely convinced that he's not wearing a wire. He explains that he is not willing to go any further for the audience; however, Carrot Top can vouch for him. The magician steps behind a privacy screen and removes the rest of his clothing, raises his arms in the air, and to the delight of the audience, spins around for Carrot Top's inspection. The magician then asks

Carrot Top if he sees anything funny… quickly modifying the question to, "Am I wearing a wire?"

But before the actual experiment begins, the magician says that he will eliminate his sense of sight by taping his eyelids shut with clear tape. The magician then reaches for the cards, accidentally knocking them off the edge of the screen, all over the floor. In an effort to help, Carrot Top begins to pick up the cards. The magician stops him, saying it's okay, because he always carries a spare. As he says this, from seemingly nowhere, or from somewhere the audience would prefer not to believe, he produces a new deck of cards inside a clear surgical rubber glove.

This deck is given to Carrot Top, who removes a random card. The magician suggests that even though he is blindfolded, Carrot Top should still keep the face of the card hidden, just in case anyone might think that he, the magician, can somehow peek. The magician then explains that he will stick out his tongue and Carrot Top is to just tap the face of the card on his tongue. Once Carrot Top does this, the magician discerns that the selected card is a red card.

Carrot Top confirms this and the magician states what is on the minds of the audience, that he had a 50 - 50 chance of being correct, so that was not all that impressive. The magician asks Carrot Top to tap again. This time the magician exclaims it's a Diamond! Carrot Top confirms this and again the magician admits that he still had a 50-50 chance. The magician asks Carrot Top to place the card on his tongue one more time. This time the magician licks all over the card. Then, in dramatic form, while pealing the tape blindfold off his eyelids, the magician explains that through his super-human sense of taste, he knows that Carrot Top's card was not just red, not only a diamond, but actually the King of Diamonds!

I am that magician, and this has been a description of a routine I developed called *"Tasteless"* as I performed it on *Penn & Teller: Fool Us*.[6] — Vinny Grosso

exposed

I'd love to think I was smart enough and had enough foresight to have planned my appearance on *Penn & Teller:*

---

[6] Penn & Teller: Fool Us - "You Dirty Rathead" (Season 3, Episode 5)

Fool Us as well as it turned out. I was not that smart; I did not have great foresight; but I am smart enough to run full speed in the direction it has taken me.

With the exception of this chapter, *exposed & FEARLESS* was written in 2014, as part of a Kickstarter campaign which also included a live show with the same title. This was followed by a motivational lecture for university students based on the book, and ultimately other such lectures. Indeed, that was my original intent, because through my motivational presentations I feel *exposed and Fearless* has the greatest potential for helping others. They offer personal satisfaction for me as well, in that they are where I feel most comfortable. The motivation and purpose for writing this book and putting on a show or lecture based on the book, was to prove through my own actions the validity of the book's theme, that through concerted effort one's fears can be overcome in pursuit of one's passion. I did that, and the ovation to my efforts has not only been gratifying, but has also validated my premise.

The stories and examples in this book are about people who remain focused, pursuing their passions, and not letting fear stop them. I wondered if my personal success qualified me to join my friends — Cesar Millan, Banachek, David Copperfield, and the others. Or was my Kickstarter experience merely one more isolated blip on my lifeline, a stand-alone occasion that I could reference in conversation that when, combined with other blips, gave the illusion that I had achieved some sort of lasting success. It must admit it was the latter, because once the goal of writing the book and doing the show and lecture was achieved, I settled back into a cushy consulting job, tour managing even more artists, and doing the occasional magic performance. But life was good... I thought.

In fact, I had fallen into the age-old trap of incidental success, the tendency to be satisfied with something short of the ultimate goal. As a result I was once again living my life exactly opposite to the order of my passions. And I wasn't inclined to do anything about it, either! I mean, why should I? Financially, I had never been better off.

I now know that I would have stayed locked into that lifestyle, settling for less than what I was capable of, if it weren't for a series of events that were to prove critical to providing me the opportunity to pursue my passion in a sustainable way. These events were to teach me that my

Kickstarter success was meant to be the beginning, not the end. It had merely opened the door. The first of these events was the decision to move to Las Vegas.

With brief exception, I have lived my entire life in a small, upstate New York town called Coxsackie. Living there can be about as fun and exciting as trying to pronounce its name. It is where my family lived, but there are also many benefits to living in a small town where people look after one another. One thing it didn't have though, was magicians or entertainers, people with passions similar to mine.

I distinctly remember the moment, hanging out with my friend Mike Mills, when he questioned why I still lived in Coxsackie. The primary benefit I touted was proximity to family, a benefit that no longer existed because my parents now spend most of their time in Florida and my siblings have moved their families out of town. Mike pointed out that with my line of work I could really live anywhere and, more importantly, I should *try* living somewhere else. Take a chance! Adventure! "Why not Las Vegas?" he suggested. "You have so many magician friends there, Brad just moved out there (Brad Sherwood, see chapter 5) and loves it." I couldn't argue with him, so I looked into it. I've never really been afraid of taking risks, so three months later I was a Las Vegas resident.

Today, I tell people my only regret is that I hadn't moved to Las Vegas earlier. It's not just an incredibly fun place to live, but also, for me, surrounded as I am by magicians and friends, people with whom I share the same passions, people who encourage and support me, it was and continues to be amazing!

Another New York magician living in Las Vegas is Jen Kramer. I have known Jen since her high school years when she was active in The Society of American Magicians youth program - The Society of Young Magicians.

One weekend when Jen's father was visiting, she invited a few friends over for brunch. Between mouthfuls, Jen was telling us about being on the television show, *Penn & Teller: Fool Us*. She had been on the previous season and it had been a great experience for her. Penn and Teller and the network folk treated her well and made every effort to help her shine, as they do for every performer on the show.

"Vinny," said Jen's father. "You should go for it." He was, in fact, perplexed that I hadn't tried before. "Just being on the show, whether or not you actually *fool* Penn and Teller, will be great for your career!"

While that last statement is true, at the time I didn't think it applied to me ...but more on that later. First let me pull back the curtain and give you some inside information about the show. The truth is that while the premise of the show is for magicians to try to fool Penn and Teller, the real benefit to professional magicians is that the show is a superb opportunity to showcase their talents.

If you are not familiar with the show, each episode features four performers. Each performer is introduced by a host, Alyson Hannigan, a brief bio video is played and then the performer comes on stage. The performer does his or her routine for Penn and Teller and the live audience. When the routine is over, the performer is interviewed by Alyson while Penn and Teller privately discuss how they think the magic was done. Penn and Teller then discuss the routine with the performer, and either make it known that they know how the magical effect was done, using references another magician will understand but that will not reveal the secret to the audience, or occasionally acknowledge that they have been fooled. If the performer succeeds in fooling them, he or she receives a trophy and an invitation to perform in one of Penn and Teller's Las Vegas shows at a later date. Each episode concludes with a performance by Penn and Teller.

Even though Penn and Teller might know one or more of the contestant magicians, they actually have no idea who will be on any given episode until the performers step on stage. The format is brilliant, connects with the audience, and offers just the right touch of suspense.

Penn and Teller are two of the greatest minds in magic, and they have been working together for over 40 years. They have seen it all and done it all. Fooling them on their TV show is quite difficult and perhaps one magician per episode will accomplish that feat. Even then, being a seasoned magician myself, I have wondered how often they are really fooled. You see, the challenge for Penn and Teller is that they essentially get one guess to say how they think an effect is done. If they're incorrect, that performer is considered a "fooler" and wins the prize. Many magic routines can be accomplished by more than one method. Penn and Teller are experienced enough that they can eliminate most methods, and usually hit the correct one. But I suspect that in some cases where they are "fooled," it was by a method that would have been their second or third choice.

In addition, some magicians deliberately try to make it look like they are using a different method than what they actually are. They drag a "red herring" across the path. In this way some have succeeded in "fooling" Penn and Teller, but in my opinion that makes for a hollow victory.

There's also another aspect to this. There are some performers who didn't "fool" Penn and Teller but actually think they did. You see, Penn and Teller's explanation doesn't have to be precise; if they're in the general area, the trick does not count as a fooler. For example, suppose the magic happens because one object is switched for another. The idea in magic is that a switch should not even be suspected. If there was a switch, and Penn and Teller recognize that, they weren't fooled – even if the actual method or subtlety for the switch is original to the performer. Some performers do not understand this and, because their method of making the switch may be unique, they believe the switch should be credited as "fooling" them.

In any case, from a professional's point of view, Penn and Teller have designed their show to be a wonderful showcase for magicians. Time and again, while acknowledging that they know how an effect was done, they have lavished praise on the magician for his or her ingenuity, skill, and performance. It is not uncommon for a routine whose method is well known to Penn and Teller to be more entertaining than a routine that fooled them. Appearing on the show is akin to appearing on the Johnny Carson Show back in the day. It is a tremendous boost to one's career regardless of whether or not Penn and Teller are fooled. Even though I was fortunate to fool them, I recognize that was just the frosting on the cake; the cake was being on the show.

To be honest, I didn't fully recognize that before I appeared on the show. I thought that if I didn't fool them, I would have failed. If that sounds a bit ungrateful or short-sighted, let me explain.

Remember that about 18 months previous I had successfully completed my Kickstarter campaign titled *exposed & FEARLESS*. Even though I was not pursuing that particular passion as, well, "passionately" as I should, I still recognized that my performing career was tied to that theme. So the question in my mind was, would fooling Penn and Teller move my career forward?

After my NYC premiere of *exposed & FEARLESS*, back in 2014, I transitioned the show into an exclusive, high-dollar, underground experience. The market was purposely limited: fewer performances, smaller audiences, higher ticket prices. In addition to individual ticket sales, it was common for any given performance to be picked up by a corporation or a wealthy individual sponsor. To use any of the routines from this exclusive show for *Fool Us* would be to diminish the value of my show because showcasing it on a national television series would eliminate the exclusivity of the experience.

Therefore, I had to come up with something new and different. What came immediately to mind was a routine only partially developed that I had performed in front of my peers as a "work in progress" at an invitation-only magic conference. I call the effect *Tasteless.* As I begin the routine, I explain that throughout my life I have been such a picky eater that many people think I have a problem. I consider it as a gift, I explain, because I have developed an incredibly fine sense of taste. I prove this by licking the face of a randomly selected card while blind folded, and determine its color, suit and value.

Even in its rough form, it had fooled many of my peers. However, as it stood, I knew it had no chance of making the cut for the *Penn & Teller: Fool Us* show, let alone stand a chance of fooling them. Beyond the method, the presentation needed a ton of work.

Working it through in my head, I realized that a minor tweak to the method would greatly transform the presentation. That minor tweak was coming up with a way to eliminate the possibility that I was being signaled the name of the card by a confederate via an electronic devise hidden under my clothes, like an FBI informant "wearing a wire." The only way to really prove this would be to strip down to my birthday suit. Clearly I could not do this in front of an audience…or could I? I remembered as a

teenager watching Penn & Teller when they came to
Proctors Theatre in Schenectady, New York. They did a
routine where they explained that when magicians
produced objects, they were actually hidden on their bodies
inside or under their costumes. To prove they were not
hiding anything, Penn & Teller stripped down behind
privacy screens observed by volunteers from the audience,
who verified that nothing was hidden.

That was brilliant! The expressions on the faces of the
volunteers were priceless! Penn & Teller really were
stripping down! They proved their point to the audience,
were funny in the process, and it was all done without
offending anyone. I thought that if I did something similar
for Penn & Teller, it would certainly accomplish the same
objective as well as subtly pay tribute to them. I also knew if
I was going to do that I had to make it my own. I could strip
down, but I wasn't either of them, and the presentation had
to be unique to me.

This minor tweak transformed my presentation into a full
on comedy routine centered around juxtaposition. If I was
going to end up naked, how should I begin in order to be as
far from naked as possible? A tuxedo! I'm not a fan of the

stereotypical magician wearing a tuxedo, and I don't believe
that Penn & Teller are either, so perhaps by stepping onstage
decked out in one, I could add the additional touch of
presenting a parody of a cheeseball magician. It kept
building from there.

As I came up with different ideas, I had one guiding
principle. Every joke, every action, had to make sense and
be completely justified in the context of "proving" that I had
an incredible sense of taste. I knew stripping naked on
stage, behind a screen or not, was going to be at least mildly
shocking and I did not want it to seem to be a gratuitous
grab for attention.

As you can see, my routine *Tasteless* (a name my friend
Steven Sokulski came up with after I added the stripping
segment) is completely different from anything I would
feature in my exclusive show.

One of the benefits of a being on *Fool Us,* whether the
performance fools Penn and Teller or not, is that the
magician is able to use the footage of the performance for
promotional purposes. I determined that in my case, a
routine in which I stripped naked was of absolutely no use

to me for my exclusive shows. I was not about to do it live, and even the video would be inappropriate for my audiences. Therefore, I felt the footage would be useless to me because it did not represent me or my show, *exposed & FEARLESS*. So for me, the real benefit would be simply to reference my appearance on my marketing materials, and it would be much better to say "fooled Penn & Teller," than say "as seen on *Penn & Teller: Fool Us.*"

So my mind set going into this was that I really did need to fool Penn and Teller. While developing the routine, I even succumbed briefly to the idea mentioned earlier of using a "red herring" to mislead the duo into guessing a method different from the one I was actually using. I thought that fooling them in that way would be sure fire.

However, prior to preparing my first audition video for the show, I discussed my ideas with two of the show's magic consultants, who also happen to be friends of mine. They cautioned me against using the red herring. They explained that it was a cheap way of "fooling" Penn and Teller and counter to the spirit of the show. I immediately saw they were right and I removed all subtleties that I thought could be misleading. This had the added advantage of motivating me to make the routine as good and as fair as I possibly could. If I was going to fool them, I was *really* going to fool them.

Along with this challenge came stress. There was so much work to be done. Most magicians on the show present polished routines with hundreds, if not thousands, of performances behind them. I had some experience with the method I was going to use, but not exactly in the way I would use it, and certainly no experience with the stripping part. This would be brand new territory for me, and I was actually still feeling my way with the presentation when I submitted the initial video of my routine for consideration. It was far from polished, to say the least; in fact it was really quite terrible. My hope was that the *effect* was good enough to be accepted for the show. Then I'd then have plenty of time to polish it.

I waited months to hear from the producers, all that time imagining how I'd improve the routine, but not really working on it, certainly not performing it. Perhaps I did not really think it would be accepted. Then, with only a month to go before they were scheduled to start taping the show, I received a phone call. They were very interested, but they had several concerns, all of which I was well aware of and had fixes already planned. However, they were not inclined to take my word for it. I didn't blame them; the video I originally sent them was really bad, so bad that a friend of mine was shocked that they were giving me a second chance to improve it.

They did, however, and I scrambled to make changes and book a performance to record new footage to send them. It was a crazy few days, and while the new footage was a lot better than the first, it was still far from a polished act. It did, however, do what was needed. I was invited to be on the show.

I had a little less than a month to polish the routine. I worked on it like crazy, not just on the routine, but also on my diet and exercise regiment. I mean – I was going to take my clothes off in front of millions of people. I didn't feel that my body was all that flattering to begin with, and a camera was only going to make it look worse! All of this wore me out. A week before the taping I was so run down I got sick, but I was on tour with Cesar Millan the five days before filming, so I couldn't even rest.

I arrived home in Las Vegas after midnight of the day that they were to film my interview and my off-stage rehearsal for the producers. I had to be ready at 8:00 AM, sick and exhausted, but with plenty of adrenaline to get me through. I have done many interviews in the past and have never been very happy with their outcome. My face never seems natural and my answers are far too verbose. I feared I was in for a long day.

For some reason I was relaxed and able to give fairly succinct answers. Maybe it was just in my head from all the exhaustion, but I finally felt good about an interview. The off-stage rehearsal went great, too. The day was capped by shooting what is called B-role footage, or color footage that would go into my introductory bio video. We shot that in David Copperfield's secret warehouse and museum. The producers wanted to highlight the fact that I was a past national president of The Society of American Magicians, a position once held by Harry Houdini, and David has arguably the world's largest Houdini collection. I'm grateful to David for his kindness in allowing me to shoot footage there.

In the few days I had before my actual performance, I caught up on my sleep and regained my health in order to be as ready for the show as possible. The night before the show I had three very close friends, Nick Lange, Mike Miller, and Mark Weidhaas, pretend to be Penn, Teller and the host, Alyson Hannigan. We went through every scenario we could think of and how I should react to each of them. I was not about to allow my tendency to be verbose in interviews diminish my performance. I was going to be ready with quick, direct, and hopefully funny comments to respond to anything thrown at me.

The morning of the show came and I talked with the producers. They had concerns about my using Alyson as a volunteer and asked if I could use the well-known comedian Carrot Top instead. I had known this might be a possibility, so I had worked a bit on how I should introduce Carrot Top. I have never cared for people who act like they're doing something impromptu when they clearly aren't. I think audiences see right through that, and I didn't want to go into the audience and just "happen" to see Carrot Top and call him up. So I came up with a quick, humorous way to introduce him from the wings and still convey that he was not "in" on the routine.

I also did an on-stage rehearsal with stand-ins for Carrot Top, Alyson, Penn and Teller. At the end of my routine I need to walk off stage. I begin the routine in a tuxedo, but end it stark naked standing behind a small privacy screen made of fogged, mostly opaque, Plexiglas. The screen is on wheels and is "U" shaped, covering my sides and front from just below the thighs to just above my mid-section. My backside is completely exposed, and when I walk off stage I turn 90 degrees, giving whoever is on stage more of a view than they probably want.

This had been the producer's idea and I went with it. After the rehearsal, however, he came up to me and said that it might make the host, Alyson, uncomfortable and that would not be funny for her or the audience. We dropped that bit, but it is important to point out that I never rehearsed an on-stage walk-off without turning 90 degrees.

To say I was nervous would be an extreme understatement! I was about to take a huge risk and be naked on TV, and if I didn't fool Penn and Teller, I was going to be devastated (again, my thinking in the moment). While I was incredibly nervous, Penn and Teller had to be incredibly tired. They had been taping two shows a day for two weeks. They are also known for despising the stereotypical cheese ball magician, the exact type of magician I appear to be when I step on stage in a tuxedo. I would need to be on stage for a short time before being announced by Alyson. Then, after what would seem an eternity, but which would be about three minutes, she would announce me and I would take just a couple of steps into place. As best as I can recall, the time I spent in the wings before being announced was the most terrifying three minutes of my life!

That all changed in a split second because of one of the kindest favors I've ever received. Teller did not know me, or anything about me. He just saw a cheese ball in a tuxedo, and I could only imagine the frightful premonitions going through his head. But he saw my nervousness, really my absolute terror masked as nervousness, and instead of expressing dismay, or trepidation about the corny magic act that might follow, he made eye contact with me, smiled, and gave me a thumbs up. I couldn't believe it! In that moment I suddenly recalled all the stories about past performers who talked about how Penn and Teller had been on their side, kind, and incredibly supportive, and I knew they were true. Suddenly the edge was gone. I could breathe. I could focus on giving the audience my best. I could overcome my fear! That is quite possibly the most gratifying moment of my entire performing career. It is certainly my most favorite.[7]

Once I got into the routine everything was a blur. I can only remember hearing the audience laugh at times and hoping they'd laugh and applaud at the end. It was then time to see if Penn and Teller had figured out how I had found the selected card. From rehearsal with my friends the night before, I had convinced myself that they would think the blindfold was fake. If so, and they would think I had seen the card, then I would have indeed fooled them, for the blindfold was real. But if they did think the blindfold was real, I was convinced that they would immediately figure out how I had discovered the value of the card, and I would have failed to fool them.

As I recall, Penn's first comment to me before he went into their theory of how I had accomplished the effect, was

---

[7] That was my understanding and feeling about the situation at the time of writing the second edition of this book. Since then I have been able to spend time with Teller and I told him this story. His recollection was a little different. He said all he remembers is Johnny Thompson, one of the consultants and judges for *Fool Us*, say through his earpiece, "You're going to like this act." Then proceeded to give me a thumbs up. For the record, this is still my favorite moment in my performing career and by an even greater margin now.

something like, "Boy! I really hope you fooled us, because this is a routine we'd like to see again in our regular Vegas show." Remember, part of the award for fooling them was to appear in that show. I say "something like" because I

honestly do not remember what he said; that's what a friend of mine who was there told me. That portion of my life is still a blur. I do remember Penn saying that he thought my blindfold was legitimate. I remember my hopes were instantly dashed, because, remember, I had convinced myself that fooling them was dependent on their thinking I could see through the blindfold. I prepared myself to listen to Penn's clever way of explaining the method without actually exposing it to the audience. He began talking about Houdini getting naked behind a screen, but I don't

remember anything else. I just "knew" that I had failed. After a little bit I threw up my hands and said, "I can't believe I got naked for this!" I took up the screen and started to shuffle off the stage.

Alyson, the host, stopped me and asked if I thought Penn and Teller knew how the effect was done. I turned back to her and said, "Yes." I can still see her face. She was dismayed, but I didn't connect the dots as to what that meant at the time. I was just upset that I hadn't fooled them, and that I had wasted time and money, and more importantly my one, great opportunity! My self-esteem dropped through the floor! Surely, it couldn't get any worse…. Wrong! Remember, I had not actually rehearsed my final exit on stage under broadcast conditions. There I was, holding the privacy screen to preserve my modesty, shuffling for the wings. My path took me in front of some very powerful lights which lit up my privacy screen like a silhouette on the blind of a bedroom window, making my privacy screen much less private! Penn leaped up from his chair, pointed at me and yelled, "You're back lit! I can see your [#!@$], I can see your [#!@$]." I was now mortified!

Just off stage, I was quickly ushered back to do a couple of pick-ups with Carrot Top. A pick-up is a reshoot of some actions to get better camera angles that would be seamlessly edited into the final cut of my segment of the show. These are not used to fake the magic trick in any way. I quickly checked the location of the perilous lights, and shuffled back, still naked, and still holding my privacy screen. They re-shot Carrot Top selecting a playing card and me revealing the card to him. Once that was over they excused

Carrot Top, but not me. I was left standing out on stage, naked, behind the privacy screen while Penn and Teller were deliberating. This took so long that Penn added to the enjoyment of the audience, and to my discomfort, by saying, "We're just trying to see how long we can keep you out here." Finally the stage manager said they had one more pick-up they'd like to do, of Penn giving me his explanation.

My heart sank below floor level. I was already depressed and mortified, and now I had to go through it all again. Penn started by telling the audience about Houdini getting naked behind a screen. Then, he surprised me by asking if he could inspect the screen. I said yes, of course, and both Penn and Teller leapt from their chairs and came charging towards me. I had nowhere to go! I couldn't very well follow instincts to run screaming from the stage. Then it hit me. They thought the screen was gimmicked! It wasn't. My rehearsal time with my friends paid off, because I had a joke all ready for this possibility. As they stepped towards me I said, "Objects behind the screen appear smaller than what they actually are." This got a great laugh. My confidence began to return and I was starting to wonder if perhaps I might have actually fooled them. Could it be?

They manhandled the screen, cameras rolling, and finally Penn slammed it and said, "There's nothing wrong with the screen!" And then the most beautiful words in the world: "You fooled us!"

I lost it! I shouted, screamed, actually, and cheered with pure joy, the kind of pure joy reserved for Christmas mornings in my youth when Santa Claus nailed it and left me the gift I had been longing for. After that outburst, I shifted back into auto drive and tapped into all the options I had worked so hard on and rehearsed, those things I would do and say, if and when. What was it I planned to do if I did fool them? Oh, yes, do it now! So I began jumping up and down, pushing the envelope of coverage provided by the privacy screen. Penn and Teller, comic geniuses that they are, went with my reaction. Each grabbed a side of the screen and raised and lowered it in unison with my jumps. The audience went hysterical!

Then the "Fool Us" trophy was lowered from where it had been hidden in the overhead grid, and Penn handed it to me. When I took it with both hands, Penn pushed it down and pulled the screen away, leaving just the trophy between the audience and me. Then it was my turn to take Penn and Teller's lead and run with it. I enjoyed every second of it!

Afterwards, I saw my friend Mike Close, who is one of the magic consultants for the show. He told me that he and Johnny Thompson, the other magic consultant, were listening in on Penn and Teller's deliberation, as they do for every routine. They knew that Penn and Teller had not figured out how I had done the routine and had given the host, Alyson, a heads up that I was going to be a "fooler." I knew that was the procedure, so when I saw Alyson looking shocked and dismayed when I told her I thought Penn and Teller knew how my trick was done, I should have realized they actually did *not* know. Mike asked me why I had given up so easily, and headed off stage so quickly. I told him it was a blur, but I figured that if they knew my blindfold was real, they knew how I did it.

Actually, at the time, I didn't think they knew my specific method, but I was not about to make an issue of that. I mentioned earlier how some magicians miss the point – if it is clear to Penn and Teller that a switch is made, for example, the precise method is not important. Now, I am an incredibly sore loser, in any kind of game or competition. I know that about myself, and I was determined to handle myself with dignity and class... well, with as much dignity and class as one can have while being naked.

Mike told me that he and Johnny had told the producers that I had misinterpreted Penn's explanation and had left the stage, but that I had, in fact, fooled them! The producers relayed this information to both Penn and Teller, and told them the footage they had of me walking off stage was footage as a non-fooler. They could wrap it there, or they could reshoot it in preparation for winning the trophy. Penn and Teller didn't hesitate. I had fooled them and they would reshoot the finish. You can imagine how I felt when Mike told me that. They clearly liked my performance and the fact that I had fooled them. Just when I didn't think I could be any happier, I received that additional boost of confidence which simply reinforced my respect and appreciation for the character of both Penn and Teller.

There is still one question I haven't answered. I said that at first I thought that the most important thing was for me to fool Penn and Teller, but that I realized later that it really didn't matter. Am I only saying this because I *did fool them?* Not at all! ...although that certainly made it more fun. You see, I didn't think I would ever use the footage because I couldn't see how it would fit with my show, *exposed & FEARLESS*. I still feel that way. It does, however, fit perfectly with my motivational lecture, *exposed & FEARLESS*. You will remember that this book is about the journeys some of my friends have taken and my observations of them along the way. My *Penn & Teller: Fool Us* performance, what it took to get there, and what it means to me going forward, is an incredibly important part of my journey. It opened a door that allowed me to see my path forward. I now begin my motivational presentation by showing the video of my performance on the Penn & Teller show. As they watch my performance, I share with my audience my experience and what it meant to me. Symbolically, I open that door and take my audience with me through that door. Together, by discussing my Penn & Teller experience, and lessons learned from the other subjects in my book, we explore a future filled with possibilities, not just for me and my friends, but for every member of my audience, discussing as we all move forward, *exposed & FEARLESS!*

Thank you, Penn & Teller, for giving me an opportunity to pursue my passion.

FEARLESS

Performing a routine in front of Penn and Teller, a live audience, and millions of viewers at home is fearful enough. The fact that Penn and Teller are trying to figure out how you are doing your effect and then give you their theory immediately after you perform is not just fearful, but intimidating as well. That, of course, wasn't enough for me. I had to do the routine naked! Some would say, I think, that took the level of fear up as many notches as it took down the level of my intelligence. I don't recommend it for everyone!!

When I first started working on the routine for *Fool Us,* I was most definitely afraid of going naked. However, after rehearsing it in my mind a few times, learning to perform the routine cold (no pun intended), that fear subsided. I simply followed my formula of experience + knowledge and it reduced my fear, as it will for you. Actually, that turned out to be the easy part. The truly fearful part of the experience was for me to put myself out there, to push the envelope, to expand my horizons. I have always wanted to be a performer, and while I have performed plenty of shows, the nature of magic is that it allows one to be lazy, if one so chooses. That is, one does not have to be polished, because the "magic" at the end can be used as a crutch. It fools the audience and the audience subconsciously forgives a less than stellar performance by the magician. As long as the trick works, the performance will be credible, the audience will applaud, and the magician fools himself into thinking that he is an entertainer. Actually, the trick was the entertainment and the magician merely a facilitator. Too often magicians settle for a *credible* performance by being lazy rather than strive for an *incredible* performance by pushing the envelope. The goal should be for the audience to applaud the magician as an entertainer who uses magic. While I knew that, I found myself in the role of the lazy magician.

I never became more cognizant of this than when I took a stand-up comedy class a few years back. Every word is so important in a stand-up routine, that eliminating, changing, or adding just one word can make an unfunny line funny, and vice versa. It's really that sensitive. Also, for the most part, comedians do not have any crutches to get applause if their dialogue is not entertaining.

True magical performers are those who entertain and would be just as entertaining without their props. They have taken care to make sure every premise and every line makes sense and fits perfectly with whatever apparatus they use to add mystery to their routines. Prior to the Penn & Teller experience I had several decent magic routines to which I had given some thought and care, but even though there was magic at the finish, none of them was really complete.

They weren't solid all the way through, good enough in their dialogue and mystery that I could be comfortable presenting them under the conditions of *Penn & Teller: Fool Us*.

To be honest, my fear was that I wouldn't be able to put together a routine worthy of the challenge. In the past I have had severe insecurities regarding my shows. The effects were based on routines I developed when I was younger that were never polished sufficiently. They were credible, but not incredible. The fact is that after performing a half-dozen of those routines in a show, I never felt satisfied; I knew they fell short. I could envision a successful show, but I was too lazy to fully develop it. Instead of working harder to fine-tune those ideas, I would move on to new ideas, which created a recurring cycle of mediocre performances.

I realized that my performance on *Penn & Teller: Fool Us* had to be exceptional; there could be nothing lazy about it. Considering how poor my first video had been, I was fearful I couldn't do it. Once I agreed to submit a new video, however, I forced myself to mentally commit to follow through regardless of the fear I felt. So it was not just a commitment to the Penn & Teller show, it was a commitment to myself. There would be no turning back. I essentially forced myself to follow through.

Some people use fear as a motivator, embracing the discomfort as a way to push forward. Others see fear as an obstacle that they must hurdle and leave behind to achieve the goal. My fear was standing between me and my passion. I reached out, firmly grasped the handle of that door of opportunity, opened it and stepped through. You can too.

parting thoughts

Throughout this book I talk about finding and pursuing your passion, not letting fear hinder that pursuit. I also share how at different moments, or "blips" in time, I have pursued my passion with some success and failed to follow through, to push on harder. I have asked myself why that has been so? Was I really pursuing a true passion if I turned away from the path forward after that moment of success? Did I allow fear to get the best of me?

Through personal reflection, I have found that I am successful when I have clear goals with deadlines over which I have no control. That is, I am unable to procrastinate or turn aside. In such cases, when I focus on goals and work as hard as I can toward their achievement, I find that things tend to fall into place. Not without hiccups and glitches, but the mindset that results from strict focus and hard work make unexpected challenges easier to meet and adjustments easier to make. This book is a result of this approach, but let me add that the final product is far different from, and better than, I think, my original concept.

Performing on *Penn & Teller: Fool Us* is another example, of course. I have shared my belief that the *Penn & Teller: Fool Us* experience opened a door to a future filled with promise.

Now I need to be honest with myself (exposed) and not be afraid to set ambitious goals (fearless). Regardless of what I have achieved, I know there is always another goal out there. What's next for you?

chapter 12

Déjà Vu

oops, I did it again

The previous chapter, entitled *Fooled Ya*, was written as an addition for the second edition of this book, which was released the day that my appearance on Season 3 of *Penn & Teller: Fool Us* aired on television. This chapter, entitled *Déjà Vu*, was written for the third edition of the book, which was released the day my appearance on Season 5 of *Penn & Teller: Fool Us*[8] aired. Yes! I did it again! So much has happened between the two appearances.

After my first appearance on Season 3, I was immediately contacted by America's Got Talent to perform my *tasteless* routine. I refused for many months; the routine was developed for Penn & Teller and the format of their television show. AGT (America's Got Talent) uses a completely different format, and I felt the routine could not be presented well. I was eventually talked into it, however, and while it was a fun experience, and AGT presented the routine as well as I could have hoped, I frankly was not prepared for the whole AGT experience. My focus was getting through that routine. It was a valuable lesson learned.

---

[8] Penn & Teller: Fool Us - "The Rematch" (Season 5, Episode 2)

I was also able to use the exposure (again, no pun intended) of *Penn & Teller: Fool Us* to book a lecture tour for magicians. When magicians lecture for other magicians, they generally share their routines, methods and theories. I had developed a lecture years ago but never did much with it. I never set concrete goals; and, in fact, I never thought anyone would be all that interested in my theories on magic.

However, now I had a routine that had fooled Penn and Teller and had generated considerable comments and speculation on my YouTube channel as to how I had accomplished it. Incorrect theories were in abundance! This gave me the confidence that maybe I did have something to offer. It also generated attendance for my lectures, and the tour was a success. I enjoyed it thoroughly, and plan to lecture in the future from time to time.

An additional benefit of my appearance on Season 3 of Penn & Teller: *Fool Us* is that I established a relationship with them and the show. If you watch Season 4, I can be seen moving a prop for my friends Fred and Bobbie Becker. I had so much fun working with them because of their excitement, passion, and commitment for making the most out of their performance. While my small part in their performance was stress free, my connection with Season 4 was not entirely without stress, however. Teller recommended me to the producers to help with one of his and Penn's routines they perform at the end of each show. This one was a classic routine of theirs called *Upside Down*, developed exclusively for television. Penn and Teller are seen doing some amazing magic, boasting how good they are while taking some fun shots at their colleagues. At the end of the routine the camera zooms out, rotates 180°, and the television audience is let in on what the live audience knew all along – Penn and Teller were hanging upside down and gravity was making every trick work!

This has always been my favorite routine of theirs. The first time I watched it I was blown away by the magic and struggled to figure out how it was possible. Then the reveal at the end – so clever and, above all else, entertaining. To be asked to help with this was an honor!

But what could I possibly do to help? The trick is very demanding from a physical standpoint, and I believe at one point Penn said on his podcast that he just didn't feel like going through that again. They asked Jenn Kramer and

AmberLynn Walker, two other magicians, to do the upside down portion while the camera would go back and forth between them and Penn and Teller. Kind of like Stunt Magicians! In addition to using two other magicians, they planned to update some of the magic effects.

It was my job to work with Jenn and AmberLynn, directing the rehearsals, and to update the magic. Rehearsals took place at Penn and Teller's warehouse, where their staff could not have been more competent and helpful. The whole process was fun! That doesn't mean it was easy; certainly not for Jenn and AmberLynn. They could only practice upside down for five to ten minutes at a time before needing a break. I got hooked up upside down once just to see what it was like. It was much more difficult than I expected. Besides the physical experience of being upside down, the effort to coordinate magic moves with gravity pulling "the wrong way" and make them appear normal (right side up) while watching yourself on a monitor that shows the mirror image of you was mind-boggling!

So stress? Well, yes. It also wasn't easy during the last days leading up to the actual taping of the episode. In the beginning we were excited and motivated by our general progress, then towards the end we had to check and double-check that all the details were correct. Jenn, AmberLynn and I certainly felt the stress of not just presenting a good routine for the audience, but also of making sure Penn and Teller were happy with their decision to entrust us with one of their signature routines.

Those are my the Penn & Teller experiences that happened *between* Season 3 and Season 5. *Déjà vu* is all about Season 3 *and* Season 5. In 2016, I had a three-week stretch that I thoroughly enjoyed in the moment because I recognized it was a once in a lifetime run of good fortune. It started with spending the Easter holiday with my entire family: parents, siblings, their spouses, and children. We all stayed at my parents' house and we all had a great time enjoying everyone's company. The following week my alma mater, Villanova University, won the NCAA Men's Basketball Tournament in spectacular fashion to be crowned National Champions. The week after that I taped my first appearance on *Fool Us*. I didn't think I had fooled Penn and Teller, but they had to tell me I was wrong – I had!

In 2018, I had another incredible three-week stretch of once in a lifetime good fortune! This time it *started* with taping my second appearance on *Fool Us,* followed by spending the Easter holiday with my family, and culminating with my alma matter winning another National Championship! To top it off, when I taped my *Fool Us* appearance, once again I was sure I had not fooled Penn and Teller, and I turned at the end of my performance and began to walk off the stage. But, déjà vu, I had! Just like last time! This time Penn called me an idiot, and they had to tape an alternative exchange between Peen and me. It was all very funny!

Déjà vu indeed!

One element of my *Fool Us* appearance that does not fall under déjà vu was my approach to the performance. I mentioned that before my Season 3 appearance I thought it was important to fool Penn and Teller, and only later realized that fooling them was not the goal; in fact, to focus on that was to miss the true point of the show.

My approach to Season 5 was all about how I could do something that would be entertaining, not just for the viewing audience, but for Penn and Teller too. I not only didn't care about fooling them, as I mentioned, I really didn't believe I had much chance of doing so. My focus was purely on presenting a fun and entertaining routine.

I pitched to the producers the idea of having a celebrity on screen, like a video chat, doing a magic trick with me. I had some ideas for the trick, but nothing concrete. We discussed possible celebrities and the producers suggested Gilbert Gottfried. I did not know Gilbert, but the producers did, and since Gilbert is a close friend of Penn and Teller, they thought there was a good chance he would agree to do it. I became a Gilbert Gottfried fan when I saw him in *Beverly Hills Cop 2*, and I always enjoyed listening to him being interviewed by Howard Stern, so I was definitely excited about the opportunity.

The producers arranged a conference call to go over the idea with Gilbert, then I jumped in with some specifics. He agreed to do it! Now the challenge became how do I make this routine as good as it can be. More often than not when I have given myself that challenge I have discovered that the answer is I can't do it, at least not on my own. One of the greatest fortunes of my life is the collection of friends I have. Their support is only equalled by their talents.

I had dinner with two of them, Brian South and Nick Lange, co-creators and co-executive producers with me on the *Worst Show in Vegas*. I shared with them the routine I was working on and told them that Gilbert had agreed to do it. Nick thought if I was going to use Gilbert Gottfried, who has one of the most recognizable voices in entertainment, that I should start with him blurred out. Genius! He also thought it would be funny if he walked away at the end and the blur didn't move, making him visible. Hilarious! Such great ideas, but they needed justification.

The next morning it came to me. The premise for using Gilbert and the blur would be that I would ask him, a friend of Penn and Teller, to sneak into their warehouse, steal a magic trick, and talk me through how to do it. Since my accomplice would be a friend of Penn and Teller, he would not want them to know it was he; so blurring him out would make sense. The added benefit was that it allowed Gilbert to read from a script. He would open the magic trick and read the "instructions." I had a short amount of time with Gilbert, so this premise really helped; he did not have to memorize lines. Of course Gilbert riffed on his own, which was exactly what we wanted, but the "instructions" served as a map of the routine for him.

After I came up with the premise, I needed to succinctly communicate it to the audience. My first draft of the script was four times longer than it needed to be. Spending a little time with my friend Brian got that cleaned up.

I was thrilled! I had a routine that I thought would surely be entertaining. That was the top objective. However, since the show is a showcase for magicians, I wanted to make the magic as strong as possible. That was the second objective, almost as important as the first. The routine was based on a classic card effect, and I just tweaked a few things, the most obvious of which was that instead of using cards, I used stuffed animal toys. This was a tweak that pleased the producers, because there tends to be a lot of card tricks on *Fool Us*. But the tweak I was most pleased with was the reason I designed for why the trick would go wrong, and consequently the way the magician would make it right at the end.

In the classic routine the magician does a card trick where he or she makes a prediction as to what the volunteer will choose by showing a single card to the audience, but not to the volunteer, and places it aside. The magician then shows several cards to the audience, but, again, not to the volunteer. What the audience sees, but what the volunteer does not know, is that all of the cards are the same as the prediction card. When the volunteer takes one card from the fan of cards just shown, it will obviously match the prediction card, to the dismay of the volunteer and the delight of the audience. In this classic effect the trick appears to go wrong, because somehow the volunteer is able to choose a different card. The magician, however, makes things right by revealing the prediction card has transformed into a match of the card the volunteer now has.

In my tweak (remember I'm using stuffed animals), Gilbert displays a box of several different animals to the audience. The instructions tell Gilbert to make a prediction of which animal the volunteer will choose and conceal it with the envelope. I have the volunteer look away as Gilbert chooses the stuffed parrot as his prediction and leans the envelope against against it, hiding it from view. I have a box full of only stuffed parrots, I display them to the audience in a manner that the volunteer cannot see. I miscall them as the other animals Gilbert had in his box so the volunteer thinks it's the same box as Gilbert's. The audience believes they are "in" on the joke. Then, reading the instructions aloud with his unique voice, He instructs the volunteer to reach into the box and remove any one of the stuffed animals. The audience is expecting the volunteer to pull out a parrot. However, he pulls out a small, stuffed gorilla! The trick has failed!

In the beginning of my routine I mention Penn & Teller's famous psychic gorilla routine as being one of my favorites. Instead of acting like the volunteer had messed with the routine, as many do in the classic version of this effect, I question Penn and Teller, wondering if they are sabotaging the effect. I do this while Gilbert goes on small tirade about my screwing up the trick. I act confused, sure that Penn and Teller are behind the failure, but then appear to piece it together. The instructions said to conceal the prediction with the envelope. I mention to Gilbert that the real prediction might be *inside* the envelope. Gilbert retrieves the envelope, opens it, and removes its contents. Inside is a piece of paper upon which is written the name of the randomly selected volunteer, and a statement that the volunteer *will select a gorilla!*

What I like about this tweak is that the volunteer doesn't appear to do anything wrong. I accuse Penn and Teller of messing with the trick; maybe it's their fault. Maybe the audience wonders about that. But then I hit on the problem. We simply misunderstood the instructions, and this leads to the surprise finish. Of course the audience is quick to appreciate that my dissatisfaction with Penn and Teller was all a sham, and that I was in control all along! As it should be; after all, I'm the magician!

In addition to a method to insure the volunteer selects a gorilla, I came up with a way to have the random volunteer's name on the piece of paper. Neither method was ground breaking, so I didn't really think the routine would fool Penn or Teller.

In the previous chapter I wrote about how some magicians try to throw Penn and Teller off the path of their method by using a "red herring," some way to mislead them, and that I did my best *not* to do that. Unfortunately or fortunately, depending on your perspective, somewhat of a red herring developed organically in this presentation. All I will say is that I had no control over it and didn't realize it was even a possibility until after the performance.

I began this chapter with the subheading *"oops, I did it again,"*[9] for a couple of reasons. The first reason for "oops" was because once again I did not think I had fooled Penn and Teller, and began to walk off, just as I had two years before. The second reason for "oops" was that although it was not my intention to take them down a path that allowed me to get another *Fool Us* trophy. I did!

My intention and focus was squarely on providing an entertaining routine. Sometimes you just get lucky. However, as I quoted Seneca at the end of chapter 2, "Luck is what happens when preparation meets opportunity."

So... I'm not giving the trophy back!

---

[9] A third reason for this subheading is because I have a crush on Britney Spears but didn't want to admit that. I figure no one reads the footnotes so it's safe here.

chapter 13

Final Thoughts

extraordinary is just a little extra added to ordinary

I have shared some stories about people I admire and respect, and who inspire me. I've tried to shed light into how they have been able to accomplish what they have based on my personal observations as I spent time with them. The fact is that they are all are ordinary people who have just done something extra that has made them extraordinary. In the last two chapters I have shared my own recent experiences. I certainly do not claim to be as exceptional, as amazing as my friends described in this book. My story, my story thus far, I should emphasize, is included because it was made possible because of the inspiration I received from these friends. I am included because you can be me, you can achieve success you never thought possible by applying the lessons learned from the chapters in this book.

In fact, we are *all* capable of doing something extra, of becoming extraordinary, and it is not because of some closely guarded secret and; we do not have to be a member of some illuminati. It really is within the limits of each of us. The secret is that it takes work. That's it – work! I love the quote, "Your ideas only work if you do." Of course, that depends on motivation.

It seems to me that true motivation comes from passion. Passion is defined as any powerful or compelling emotion or feeling. To me the most important word in that definition is the word "compelling." When you are compelled to do something, you cannot resist doing it. You do it! My friend Jen Kramer and her father rekindled my passion over brunch that day in Las Vegas, rekindled it to the point that I could not resist going forward. I was compelled to do so.

If you find your passion, do not resist pursing it. Allow your self *to be compelled* to pursue it. If your passion is strong enough, you will be unable to resist its pursuit. That is the kind of motivation we need, you and I. As long as the passion lasts, the motivation will be enduring.

Motivation regarding something we simply want to have is not as strong. It is often short-lived and is easily deterred. An example of this might be weight loss. How many people do we know who struggle with this? Perhaps ourselves? "I want to lose weight!" "I am determined to lose weight!" "I am determined to exercise and be healthy!" Those are forceful statements, but do they represent passion? If a person has a passion to live a healthy lifestyle, they will. They will be compelled to do so.

My own father is a good example. My father had a heart attack at the age of 35. He was a smoker, and did not take care of his body as he should have. As he recovered from the heart attack, fitness became his passion. He exercised daily, not because he had a desire to lose weight, or reach a certain weight, but because he had a passion to be fit. He quit smoking immediately. Why? Because his passion for being healthy trumped any desire he had to have a cigarette. He lives that passion to this day, 35 years later!

Without passion motivation becomes a fleeting thing. When a goal is achieved the motivation to achieve may well be diminished, perhaps even lost. Over time the goal is lost, as well. If your passion is to learn to and play the piano, you will play the rest of your life. If your goal is to learn to play the piano, you may or may not be playing it ten years from now. You may or may not learn to play, for that matter.

You have heard people talk about the difference between wants and needs. It is a popular concept in planning personal finances and budgets, but it also applies to goals. A "want" is something you would like to have. A "need" is something you must have. Needs are passions.

The people we have learned about in this book are passionate about what they do. As a result they have achieved considerable success and fame in their respective fields. Their passion is the driving force that keeps them focused. It is not a want, it is not even a desire, it is a need. I understand that kind of passion, and it drives me forward.

At the end of chapter one I mentioned that I had an eye exam. The doctor told me I had great vision, but trouble focusing, and that my brother wondered if the doctor was diagnosing my eyes or my life. I have been very fortunate in my life. I have had many wonderful experiences and have been successful in several areas. But, in fact, I have been serving my wants, my desires, and am only now working to serve my passion.

I have yet to be extraordinary, but this book, and the endeavors I am involved in that relate to this book, are part of my quest to be so. My passion lies in performing whether it be a lecture or a show. I wrote in the first printing of this book that I was just at the threshold of my pursuit of this, and that it was an exciting place to be. In subsequent and present printings I write that my appearances the *Penn & Teller: Fool Us* show opened the door and allowed me to step across that threshold. My passion compels me to pursue it with every fiber of my being.

By opening the lives of extraordinary people, exposing the inner workings, desires and passions, wants and needs, I hope their experiences will have the same effect on you as they have had on me. Their lives are directly tied to my passion, and their lives serve as motivation for me. And hopefully my own story as it has unfolded so far will add a little to that motivation for you as well.

the courage to set aside your fears

Throughout this book I say that no one is really fearless; that is, without fear. Fear exists in all of us. The real question is, how do we react to fear? How do we deal with it? A person truly without fear will take a fearful situation head on, and, as in the case of our friend the wolf in chapter three, may very well lose a leg. Conversely, a fearful person will often avoid situations even where clearly no fear is warranted. Being fearful may very well prevent you from achieving something great.

When speaking about fear the word "courage" comes to my mind, action in spite of fear, in the face of physical or emotional danger. A courageous person is one who is aware of the danger, understands the risks, but values the potential outcome of action taken enough to go forward, to confront both the danger and the fear. A courageous person respects fear while refusing to let it control them.

Every person we have discussed in this book had to overcome fear of one kind or another, as have I. Among other things, we learn from them that what is fear for one person may not apply to another. I hope we have learned not to judge, but rather to benefit from the analysis. At the beginning of this project I discovered one of my passions was to find myself, to find a direction in life about which I could feel as much passion as my subjects do about the directions of their lives, and to analyze the role fear plays in my life and learn how to put it aside at the appropriate times.

At the close of this edition of *exposed & FEARLESS* I find myself well on the path. I see better how to pursue and achieve goals related to my passion. I am better able to define my fears and have developed strategies to tackle them. For this I thank my friends who so generously allowed a part of their life stories to appear in this book. Each of them exemplifies the late President Franklin Delano Roosevelt's memorable declaration made during his March 4th, 1988 inaugural address, as profound today as it was then, "The only thing we have to fear is fear itself!"

I hope that you have been touched by the stories of these remarkable people. I hope that you have been motivated to look at your own lives, to seek out those pursuits for which you can change interest to desire, and then to passion. For with passion, you can achieve greatness.

acknowledgements

The first edition of this book was funded through
Kickstarter and thus no other edition would have been
possible without all the support received from:

Bill Sales
Brian South
Dal Sanders
Ralph Mancuso
Lisa Juliano

Michael Mills
Margaret & Hugh Quigley
Frank & Dominica Annese
Michael & Sandra Grosso
Arndt Michael
Celeste Grosso & Ely Nathan
Richard Hinze
Jim & Diane Gargiulo
Iris & Jerry Detter
Kevin Jones
Randy Levinson
Stephen Hindmarsh

Daniel Quigley
Rebekah South
Cheryl & Michael Grosso
Cristin Soucek Watts
Madeline Grosso
Patricia Thompson
Scott Rogers
Mike Miller
Tricia Cornish
Jeremey Dudley
Coleen Grosso
Maurice Grosso
Eric DeCamps
Veronica Saunders
Andres Ravenna
Alan Jones
Christine Vrtaric

Harshad & Bharti Patel, Joseph Fontana, Andrew Bartels, Eugene Soucek, Stephanie Beach, Lynda Foley, Steve Farmer, Paul Carpenter, Doug Thornton, Shigeru Tashiro, Simone Marron, Paul Perrella, Jerry Wallace, Justin Evdokimoff, Kevin Sowizrol, Michael Tallon, Matthew Jones, Laurel Mascia, John Craig Dillon, Judy Sickles, John Zeiser, Terry Wing.

Matthew Carpenter, SJ Kahng, Ed Brewer, Ben Watson, Michael Jaffe, Briana Lohhne, Sean Andrechak, Karen Winters, Edward Thomas, Diane Pittelli, David Adamovich, Gary LaDue, Nicole Pearson, David Goodsell, Cheryl Pauly, Julie Ravenel, David Resseguie, John Bobik, Casey Harris, Holly Grosso, Mike Norden, Joe Tarquinio, Rachel McNellis, Randy Meppelink.

John Reid, Sharon Nuanes, Donna Mancuso, Mark Jeros, Rosa Bitussi, Michael Fallon, Michael Grossi, James Scheer, Allison Faul, Jeff Quinn, James O'Keefe, Mike Hawkins, Danielle Brandt.

Michael Wojciak, Brandon Heston, Michael Dardant, Brian Scott Ambrosch, Steve Rentz, Gregory Harris, Dennis Holgado, Will Fern, Tim Gaffney, Monica Manley, Stuart Rudnick, Debbie Rivers, Benjamin Farber, Micoy Gordie, David Kinze, Suzanne Hazelton, John Apperson.

David Margolin, Joseph Zompetti, Steve Marshall, Stephanie Wagner, Kaitlyn Melcher, Lynda Hacking, Elaine Scarpelli, Jeremiah Bridges, Elena Murphy, Judy Carpenter, Nicole Miller, William Kelley, Carl Seagren, John Murphy, Rebecca Susi, Ian Rich, Marc DeSouza, Judy Sutherland, Sue Rae Cramer, Eric Yip, Daniele Galante, Chandra Jessee, Curtis Hickman, Tony Swindlehurst, Miles Matton, Felipe Garcia de Godoi, TJ, Brendan, Anthony Gioe, Michael Squires, Rod Chow, Mark Weidhaas, Diana Brito-Diaz, Lyn Dillies, Justin Levy, Steven Allen's girlfriend, Daniel Sclare, Chris Urban, Kayla Drescher, Christopher A. Jablonski, Todd Neufeld, Norman Rosen, Leon Higley, David Caserta, Sandee Young, Warren, Kelly Turley, William Karabin, Mathew McGivern, Stephen Hill, Cameron Owen, Dan Manson, Ed Kowalczewski, Jonathan Cohn, Ailis Fitzgerald, Justin Burr, Dave Klaiber, Christopher Weed, Joe Vecciarelli, Jay Gorham, Philip Vanderbilt Brady, Michael Roth, Chrstopher Bontjes, Billy Hsueh, Rod Shipley, Eric J, Melina Bischoff, Michelle Adriano Soroka, Kristi Carbone, Jessica Luberda, Suasan Eyed, Keith Moehring. Brad Jacobs, Diane Gulyas, Gazido Gaming.

Tim Jackson, Abe Carnow, Jason Murphy, Linda Correll, John Gyllenhaal, Paul, Sponaugle, Wee Kien Meng, LR Williams, Richard Mindel, Miranda Celeste Hale, Rosalind Chan, Stephanie Turner, Karen Gattney.

Joan Caesar, Mia Grosso, Sarah Grosso, Casey, Anne Wojtkowiak Weidhaas,

Michael R, Kristen Nicolazzo Lazuka, Johnna Murphy, Mykel Zimmermann, Jade Brieanne, Brian Bickersmith, Jordan Bischoff.

The kickstarter project would not have been possible without the help from:

Brian & Rebekah South

and it would not have been a success without the help from:

Ricky Brandon
Michael Grosso, Jr
Rick Hinze
Steve Marshall
Wee Kien Meng
Michael Mills
Ian Rich
Scott Rogers
Matt Schick

about the author

Vinny Grosso is a professional magician, one of just a few to have fooled Penn & Teller twice on their television series *Penn & Teller: Fool Us*. He has been featured on *America's Got Talent* and in 2011 served as National President of The Society of American Magicians. Vinny is also a member of London's Magic Circle and has achieved its highest level, Member Inner Magic Circle with Gold Star.

In addition to speaking and performing corporate events throughout the US, Europe & Asia, in 2006 Vinny volunteered for two overseas tours performing for our troops through Armed Forces Entertainment.

Performing magic has always been a passion of Vinny's, but it's just one of his many dimensions. He remains active tour managing artists from comedians to authors to television personalities. He is the co-creator and executive producer of the *Worst Show in Vegas*. As a mechanical engineer he has two patents, a software company based on a patented technology and consults.

exposed & FEARLESS is also motivational talk and live show where many of the stories and themes from the book are brought to life. For more information please visit:

vinnygrosso.com

26976419R00120

Made in the USA
San Bernardino, CA
24 February 2019